Putting the Practices Into Action

Putting the Practices Into Action

Implementing the Common Core Standards for Mathematical Practice K–8

Susan O'Connell
John SanGiovanni

HEINEMANN
Portsmouth, NH

Heinemann
361 Hanover Street
Portsmouth, NH 03801–3912
www.heinemann.com

Offices and agents throughout the world

The authors and publisher wish to thank those who have generously given permission to reprint borrowed material:

Excerpts from *Common Core State Standards* © Copyright 2010. National Governors Association Center for Best Practices and Council of Chief State School Officers. All rights reserved.

Cover photographs (clockwise from top right corner): © Comstock/Getty Images/ HIP; © HMH/HIP; © HMH/HIP; © Photodisc/Getty Images/HIP; © Victoria Smith/HMH/HIP

Cataloging-in-Publication Data is on file with the Library of Congress.
ISBN: 978-0-325-04655-6

Editor: Katherine Bryant
Production editor: Sonja S. Chapman
Typesetter: Kim Arney
Cover and interior designs: Monica Ann Crigler
Manufacturing: Steve Bernier

Printed in the United States of America on acid-free paper
17   16   15   EBM   5   6   7

For the newest additions to our family,
Blake Olivia and Molly Kathleen, with love
S.O.

To my parents for
encouragement, love, and support
J.S.

Contents

Acknowledgments

Many thanks to the following students who contributed work samples or allowed their photographs to appear in this book: Ryan Balkaran, Chris Bauers, Jenny Bonilla, Isabel Centers, Aislinn Coghlan, Braedon Coghlan, Makayla Dizon, Papa Frempong, Evann Jackson, Aria Jarsocrak, Matthew Maher, Linda Mallonee, Swarna Nehumani, Rosalie Rosenberg, Annie Schinkai, Sydney Schinkai, James Schmidt, Deryn Schoenfelder, Kelby Schoenfelder, Oscar Schoenfelder, Nick Stitely, Ryan Tracey, and Ava Welsh.

We greatly appreciate the collaboration of our colleagues as we gathered materials for this book, in particular the following teachers, math coaches, and supervisors who welcomed us into their classrooms or shared their insights with us: Connie Conroy, Michelle Glenn, Jason McCoy, Kay Sammons, Kristen SanGiovanni, and Joanne Scheler.

We are extremely grateful to Katherine Bryant, our Heinemann editor, for her guidance and personal attention throughout the development of this book.

Introduction

Another set of math standards? With anxiety immediately rising, we open the standards document to take a look at the Common Core State Standards in Mathematics. We briefly glimpse the Standards for Mathematical Practice that appear at the beginning of the standards document but then quickly move past those standards to zero in on the "real standards"—the content to be taught. After all, we need to know what content is deemed important at each grade level. What will we teach? When do we introduce certain skills and concepts? We naturally gravitate toward the content to be taught; after all, *we* were taught mathematics through a content-driven approach, and math is all about content, right?

But disregarding the Standards for Mathematical Practice has a dramatic effect on our efforts to understand and address the Common Core State Standards. The Standards for Mathematical Practice highlight the level to which math content must be known, focusing on the application, reasoning, communication, and representation of the content. A deeper understanding of these eight Practices enables us to envision what it means for our students to be mathematically proficient and to select teaching practices that shift our teaching from a focus on content to a focus on application and understanding. The Standards for Mathematical Practice are actually the heart and soul of the Common Core State Standards.

FACING YET ANOTHER SET OF STANDARDS

As math standards have changed over the past several decades, we have attempted to adapt and adjust to each new set of expectations. We have reflected on what is important to teach and how we should best teach it. We have struggled with finding instructional strategies that meet the new standards and with ways to prepare our students for the changing assessments that measure these new standards. It has seemed like an ever-changing process, but a closer look at the standards movement helps us see that it has truly been an evolution rather than a series of disjointed efforts. The Common Core State Standards (CCSS) can be best understood as part of this evolution instead of viewed as "yet another set of standards."

Over the past several decades, math standards have emerged to guide us in our goal of developing mathematically proficient students. Arguably the most difficult aspect of the standards movement has been the recent emphasis on math processes, or practices, that elevate math teaching from simply requiring students to memorize facts and formulas and find correct answers. The new higher-level goals require our students to reason, apply, connect, and truly understand math skills and concepts.

The Common Core State Standards continue this emphasis on mathematical thinking and reasoning through the Standards for Mathematical Practice. Effectively implementing the CCSS depends on a deep understanding of these practice standards, as they underscore the goals for students and influence our teaching Practices. But how do they relate to what we have done in the past? How are they alike or different from past math standards? How do they look in a math classroom? How can we best incorporate them into our teaching? This book clarifies and illustrates the CCSS Standards for Mathematical Practice.

WHAT ARE THE STANDARDS FOR MATHEMATICAL PRACTICE?

Mathematically proficient students blend their knowledge of math content with their ability to apply that knowledge to solve problems, communicate math ideas, justify solutions, model math concepts, and reason to make sense of mathematics. The CCSS Standards for Mathematical Practice are the keys to these higher-level goals. These Mathematical Practices elevate our students' learning from knowledge to application. They bring rigor to our math classrooms. They are the standards that ensure an understanding of math, focus on the development of reasoning, build mathematical communication, and encourage modeling and representation. These Practices cannot be learned in quiet math classrooms filled with drill-and-practice activities. This level of thought must be developed in language-based classrooms filled with explorations and discussions about math concepts. No matter how much content is "covered" in math class, students are not mathematically proficient without attention to these standards.

A brief look at these standards, as shown in Figure 0.1, illustrates why they are a critical component of math proficiency.

▸ Standard 1 highlights the skills and attitudes required to become an effective problem solver.

▸ Standard 2 focuses on students' abilities to see the connection between real situations and symbolic representation and to accurately represent problems with quantities and symbolic representations.

Figure 0.1 *The Standards for Mathematical Practice*

1. Make sense of problems and persevere in solving them.

2. Reason abstractly and quantitatively.

3. Construct viable arguments and critique the reasoning of others.

4. Model with mathematics.

5. Use appropriate tools strategically.

6. Attend to precision.

7. Look for and make use of structure.

8. Look for and express regularity in repeated reasoning.

▸ Standard 3 focuses on students' abilities to make conjectures and justify conclusions.

▸ Standard 4 emphasizes that mathematically proficient students model math situations with diagrams, manipulatives, tables, graphs, and equations and apply math to solve real-world problems.

▸ Standard 5 highlights students' abilities to select and use appropriate tools to solve problems.

▸ Standard 6 centers on the need for precise communication about math, as well as accurate computation.

▸ Standard 7 highlights the abilities of students to recognize the structure of math through its patterns and properties.

▸ Standard 8 focuses on the abilities of mathematically proficient students to notice repetition in mathematics and use observations and reasoning to find shortcuts or generalizations.

These eight Practices call attention to what it means to be mathematically proficient, to go beyond simply memorizing facts and formulas. When our students experience mathematics through these Practices, they have repeated opportunities to make sense of the ideas and to build a deeper understanding of skills and concepts. Reflecting on these Practices, and discovering ways to integrate them into our content teaching, ensures that students have optimal experiences in our math classrooms and emerge with solid skills that are indispensable as they continue to explore mathematics at higher levels.

HOW THIS BOOK WILL HELP YOU

Mathematics is not just about content. Through attention to the CCSS Standards for Mathematical Practice, content is elevated to application and understanding. This book examines the CCSS Standards for Mathematical Practice and ultimately provides an in-depth understanding of these standards. The greater our understanding, the easier it will be to integrate these Practices into our teaching and ensure that our students develop these critical skills.

We explore each of the eight Practices through explanations, vignettes, and suggested classroom activities. The vignettes and classroom activities range from grades K–8. In order to highlight the connections between the Practice standards and the content standards you will notice the inclusion of content standard numbers next to many of the vignettes and student tasks (i.e., 1.OA.3, indicating Grade 1, Operations and Algebraic Thinking, Standard 3, or 6.EE.2, indicating Grade 6, Expressions and Equations, Standard 2). In addition, we have included side notes to indicate connections to other Practice standards, as many of the activities integrate several Practices. These references will help you visualize the ways in which content and practice are addressed concurrently.

We also share a wealth of practical ideas and activities that can be quickly integrated into your existing math program. These include sample classroom activities, suggested teacher questions, helpful teaching tips, and formative assessment ideas. At www.heinemann.com/putting-the-practices-into-action, you will find additional online resources to help you integrate these into your classroom. Images in this book will help you identify which of these online resources best meet your needs.

Focusing on these Standards for Mathematical Practice requires a change in some of our teaching practices, and change becomes easier when we are able to reflect on why and how we might change, in addition to brainstorming ways in which to change. In order to support individuals who want to reflect on their reading—or Professional Learning Communities who choose to study these practices together—this book provides study group questions to promote reflection, to prompt thinking, and ultimately, to facilitate change.

For several decades we have been pondering and refining our expectations of what students should learn while searching for the most effective teaching practices to efficiently move our students toward mathematical proficiency. Today's Common

Core State Standards are the most recent step toward that goal. The CCSS Standards for Mathematical Practice present a roadmap for the development of mathematically proficient students. It is certainly a challenging goal, but a doable one and one that is centered on what is best for our students. This book will be *your* roadmap to implementing the CCSS Standards for Mathematical Practice. The explanations, examples, activities, and suggestions are intended to guide you to a deeper understanding of the Practice standards so your classroom is filled with students who reason, apply, and truly understand mathematics.

CHAPTER 1

The Evolution of Standards-Based Teaching

So what led us to these Common Core State Standards? Understanding the evolution of the standards-based movement helps us recognize ways that we have already changed our expectations of students, our understanding of what it means to be mathematically proficient, and our insight into effective teaching practices in mathematics. Most important, it focuses us on where to go from here.

Many of us do not recall being taught mathematics through a standards-based approach. Math was a series of topics, skills to memorize, chapters in a book. Our teachers distributed worksheets and taught lessons, then tested our ability to identify or compute. We learned to add, subtract, multiply, and divide fractions, simplify fractions, and find equivalent fractions, but our knowledge and skills often ended there. We did not focus on a deep understanding of fractions, or an ability to apply fraction concepts to problem situations, or even an understanding of how these fraction concepts connected to other math concepts. Being good at math was measured by correct answers that could often be found by applying a memorized formula or algorithm. As math educators attempted to define what it meant to be mathematically proficient, the importance of thinking, applying, and understanding began to creep into conversations. Were students who could remember formulas or memorize algorithms truly mathematically proficient, or were there other skills that were necessary? Was the correct answer the ultimate goal of mathematics, or did we expect a greater level of competence?

In 1989, the National Council of Teachers of Mathematics (NCTM) published the *Curriculum and Evaluation Standards for School Mathematics*, sparking a standards-based approach to mathematics education. The NCTM contended that standards in mathematics would: ensure that students received quality experiences in classrooms, clearly articulate math goals, and promote change in the teaching of mathematics (NCTM 1989). The first four standards focused on processes (see Figure 1.1) and were followed by a series of content standards, which focused on content skills such as number and number relationships, geometry, measurement, and statistics and probability.

For the first time, mathematical processes were elevated to essential expectations, changing our view of math to encompass more than just content. The goal now was to apply, communicate, make connections, and reason about math content rather than to simply compute. This standards document also called for increased attention to problem solving, discussion, and justification of thinking. It decreased attention on rote practice, rote memorization of rules, and teaching by telling.

But NCTM's delineation of content expectations and process standards posed a challenge for math educators. These standards valued higher-level thinking, application, and communication, and most of us had not learned math in that way. While some teachers embraced these process standards and the subsequent changes in their math teaching, others of us did not know how to change or understand *why* we should change.

Perhaps the most compelling case for accepting the process standards was the changes that began appearing in student assessments as states began to align their assessments with these standards. Many state and district assessments became saturated with problem-solving tasks that required reasoning, with some even including constructed-response questions in which students had to explain processes and justify their answers. In those states, the process standards took on new meaning as teachers prepared students for these new, higher-level assessments.

Figure 1.1   *The first four NCTM standards highlighted mathematical processes.*

1. Mathematics as Problem Solving

2. Mathematics as Communication

3. Mathematics as Reasoning

4. Mathematical Connections

REFINING THE STANDARDS

In 2000, NCTM released *Principles and Standards for School Mathematics: An Overview*, which continued to strengthen the vision of mathematics as a blend of content and process, further explaining and sharing examples of standards-based teaching. The standards from the *Curriculum and Evaluation Standards* took on a new look as they evolved into five content standards that outlined expectations related to the content of mathematics and five process standards that identified and described expectations related to the critical processes that contribute to mathematical proficiency (see Figure 1.2).

While the content standards focused on familiar math content, each content strand (number and operations, algebra, geometry, measurement, data and probability) was now a PreK–12 standard, with specific expectations at various grade bands (PreK–2, 3–5, 6–8, 9–12). These content standards focused on higher-level skills characterized by such verbs as *develop, explore, describe,* and *examine* rather than the more traditional math tasks of *compute, identify,* or *memorize.* These content standards provided a progression for critical math content and challenged a depth of understanding.

The process standards also became more focused in this revised standards document, highlighting five critical processes through which our students learn mathematics:

- ▶ *Problem Solving* became the overarching process standard, challenging our students to apply the math skills and concepts learned in each content area.

- ▶ *Communication* emphasized that our students process and refine ideas through talking and writing about them.

Figure 1.2 *The National Council of Teachers of Mathematics' Standards value both content and process.*

CONTENT STANDARDS	PROCESS STANDARDS
Number and Operations	Problem Solving
Algebra	Communication
Geometry	Representations
Measurement	Reasoning and Proof
Data and Probability	Connections

- *Representations* brought attention to multiple ways in which our students represent math ideas and show what they know about math.

- *Reasoning and Proof* emphasized the importance for our students to go beyond answers and algorithms and be able to reason and defend their mathematical thinking.

- *Connections* elevated mathematics to a study of intertwined content rather than a series of isolated skills and emphasized the need for our students to see connections among and between math ideas in order to deeply understand math concepts.

These processes were seen as integral to the teaching and learning of all math concepts. Whether students were learning about numbers, geometry, or data, our challenge was to provide experiences for them to explore that content through these processes and to support them in developing their skills with these processes. We were challenged to have our students solve problems or communicate their thinking as a way to better understand the math they were learning, but also so they would develop their process skills and become better problem solvers and communicators. With content taught through these processes, students would have classroom experiences that challenged them to apply, communicate, reason, represent, and connect math ideas in order to become truly proficient mathematicians (O'Connell 2007b).

In 1998, the National Research Council established a committee to review and synthesize pertinent research on math teaching and learning in grades K–8. The goal was to provide research-based recommendations for teaching practices, curriculum development, and further research. The project was sponsored by the National Science Foundation and the U.S. Department of Education and resulted in the publication *Adding It Up: Helping Children Learn Mathematics* (2001). This publication introduced five strands of mathematical proficiency:

- Conceptual understanding—comprehension of mathematical concepts, operations, and relations

- Procedural fluency—skill in carrying out procedures flexibly, accurately, efficiently, and appropriately

- Strategic competence—ability to formulate, represent, and solve mathematical problems

- Adaptive reasoning—capacity for logical thought, reflection, explanation, and justification

▶ Productive disposition—habitual inclination to see mathematics as sensible, useful, and worthwhile, coupled with a belief in diligence and one's own efficacy. (NRC 2001)

These five interconnected strands relate to all math content. And these five strands have a tremendous effect on how students become proficient in math, the instructional practices we use to develop math proficiency, and the methods used in teacher education (NRC 2001). Again, the emphasis was on the development of thinking, understanding, and application. These strands of mathematical proficiency would later impact the development of the Common Core State Standards.

Meanwhile, the NCTM continued its standards efforts with the publication of *Curriculum Focal Points for Prekindergarten through Grade 8 Mathematics: A Quest for Coherence* (NCTM 2006). Through this document, math content shifted from grade bands to specific grade levels and provided a narrower focus by identifying the most important math topics at each grade level. The *Curriculum Focal Points* extended the *Principles and Standards* and were intended to guide decisions about curriculum development by outlining the critical math topics by grade level. With these focal points the standards movement continued to evolve.

ESTABLISHING COMMON GOALS

States began moving toward standards-based teaching at different paces. They developed their own standards, generally guided by the NCTM Standards, and then developed assessments to match their standards. Would the ability to collaborate between states and share the development of standards and assessments yield stronger standards and more effective assessments? In 2010, the *Common Core State Standards* (CCSS) were published by the National Governors Association Center for Best Practices and Council of Chief State School Officers (2010). The Common Core State Standards provide consistency across states in the teaching of mathematics and provide a common core of standards for math proficiency. This state-led initiative is built on the previous standards work of the National Council of Teachers of Mathematics.

MAKING SENSE OF THE NEW STANDARDS

The Common Core State Standards and the NCTM Standards share commonalities, such as a curriculum focused on big ideas, with skills and concepts at one grade level or grade band building on the ideas of the previous grade level or band (NCTM

Figure 1.3 *The Common Core State Standards for Mathematical Practice were influenced by both the NCTM Standards and the Strands of Mathematical Proficiency, as noted in the chart.*

CCSS STANDARDS FOR MATHEMATICAL PRACTICE	CORRELATION TO NCTM MATH PROCESS STANDARDS	STRANDS OF MATHEMATICAL PROFICIENCY
Make sense of problems and persevere in solving them.	Problem Solving	Strategic competence
Reason abstractly and quantitatively.	Representation Communication Reasoning and Proof Problem Solving	Adaptive reasoning
Construct viable arguments and critique the reasoning of others.	Reasoning and Proof Communication Representation	Conceptual understanding Adaptive reasoning
Model with mathematics.	Representation Communication	Strategic competence Conceptual understanding
Use appropriate tools strategically.	Problem Solving Reasoning and Proof	Conceptual understanding Procedural fluency
Attend to precision.	Communication Representation	Procedural fluency Conceptual understanding
Look for and make use of structure.	Reasoning and Proof Problem Solving Representation	Adaptive reasoning Productive disposition
Look for and express regularity in repeated reasoning.	Reasoning and Proof Representation Communication	Adaptive reasoning Conceptual understanding Productive disposition

2010). The CCSS and NCTM Standards value both content and process. The CCSS emphasize that the content standards should be blended with their Standards for Mathematical Practice, which are closely related to NCTM's Math Process Standards (NCTM 2010) and the National Research Council's Strands of Mathematical Proficiency (NRC 2001). All three documents embrace practices that are interconnected and that build understanding, reasoning, and application (see Figure 1.3).

Throughout this book, we acknowledge the positive changes that have been made in the movement toward standards-based teaching. We reflect on past efforts to align our teaching with the NCTM Math Process Standards as we aspire to better understand and implement the CCSS Standards for Mathematical Practice. And we continue to refine our understanding of mathematical proficiency as we explore ways to create standards-based math classrooms in which our students are able to understand and apply a wide range of math skills and concepts.

CHAPTER 2

Exploring Standard 1: *Make Sense of Problems and Persevere in Solving Them*

WHY PROBLEM SOLVING?

As we examine the first Standard for Mathematical Practice, we may find ourselves wondering, "Why problem solving?" In looking back on our own experiences as math students, we may recall computation as the main focus. A page in our math textbook probably contained 20–30 computations, with maybe one or two word problems at the bottom of the page. Many teachers report that they received As and Bs in math despite never understanding *how* to solve problems. And now the ability to solve math problems is the first standard! This attests to our belief that being able to do computations alone does not equate to math proficiency. Our new definition of proficiency includes knowing when, why, and how to apply calculations to situations. The practice of solving problems is critical to math success.

UNDERSTANDING THE STANDARD

The ability to solve problems by applying varied math skills is what makes our students effective mathematicians. This standard focuses on the development of essential skills and dispositions for becoming an effective problem solver, including:

1. An understanding of the problem-solving process and how to navigate through the process from start to finish

2. A repertoire of strategies for solving problems and the ability to select a strategy that makes sense for a given problem

3. The disposition to deal with confusion and persevere until a problem is solved.

UNDERSTANDING THE PROBLEM-SOLVING PROCESS

Problem solving is not an algorithm to be practiced or a fact to be memorized. Effective problem solvers decide—for each unique problem—what is being asked, what is important to consider, an appropriate path to the solution, and the reasonableness of their actions. Problem solvers think about their own thinking (metacognition) so they are better able to regulate and modify their thinking. They plan ways to approach a task, select appropriate tools, evaluate their own progress, and revise their actions.

The work of George Polya (1957) identified critical steps in this process, which have since been restated and refined in a variety of ways. The following questions highlight important steps in the thinking process:

What is the problem asking?

How should I begin?

Where is the necessary data?

What should I do with that data?

Did my plan work?

Does my answer make sense?

Do I need to go back and try a different strategy?

To support our students, we identify, discuss, and move toward making this process automatic, so they are then able to focus on other aspects of the complex task of solving problems.

DEVELOPING STRATEGIES

When it is time to devise a plan for solving problems, what do your students do? Do they have a repertoire of strategies from which to choose? Have they explored varied problems to see the many ways they might be solved? Have they discussed alternate ways to solve problems, to expand their thinking? Do they recognize familiar problems and determine how they might solve a given problem?

Simply knowing how to proceed through the stages of solving a problem is not enough. Our students must determine a strategy to help them solve problems, and that strategy will vary with each problem. Once our students identify the question and pinpoint the necessary information, they must decide on a plan that will lead them to the answer. While all textbooks mention and provide a few problems related to strategies such as Choosing Operations, Drawing Pictures, Making Tables, or Working Backward, the underlying skills are actually quite complex thinking skills (see Figure 2.1) that require more attention and discussion (O'Connell 2007b).

Strategy teaching is a blend of student exploration and direct teaching. Highlight and discuss students' approaches at every opportunity, especially when they lead to insights about effective problem solving. But it is also okay to introduce students to strategies (e.g., constructing tables as a way of organizing data). Many students would never think of these approaches on their own, but they come to understand and use them effectively. Our students need ongoing experience in applying these strategies, with particular emphasis on how and when to apply them and why they work for a particular problem.

BUILDING A PROBLEM-SOLVING DISPOSITION

Many students become easily frustrated when solving math problems. Anxiety, stemming from self-doubt about their abilities or a fear of failure, blocks their progress.

Am I able to do this?

What if I get stuck?

What if it takes me too long to get the answer?

What if my idea doesn't work?

What if my answer is wrong?

Believing it's possible to solve a problem, recognizing that confusion is part of the process, and discovering that persistence pays off are all components of a positive problem-solving disposition. This disposition allows our students to self-monitor, checking the reasonableness of their approaches and solutions and modifying their course of action, without becoming frustrated, anxious, or discouraged.

Figure 2.1   *This chart identifies some of the underlying thinking skills for common problem-solving strategies.*

STRATEGY	UNDERLYING THINKING SKILL(S) What students really need to know!
Choose an Operation	Understand the meaning of operations Build appropriate equations to represent problem situations
Draw a Picture	Visualize problem situations Use models to represent problems Analyze models to gain insight into problems
Find a Pattern	Recognize the importance of looking for connections between numbers Identify patterns that lead to solutions
Make a Table	Organize data to more easily identify patterns and functions that lead to solutions Continue a pattern or apply a function to find a solution
Guess and Check	Employ trial-and-error thinking Utilize number sense to move closer to an answer Make adjustments during the problem-solving process, based on mathematical reasoning
Make an Organized List	Identify a starting point and move systematically toward a solution Create a model (e.g., organized list, tree diagram) to organize confusing information and simplify a problem
Use Logical Reasoning	Organize confusing information to simplify a problem Make inferences to solve a problem Draw conclusions based on clues Identify if/then or cause/effect relationships
Work Backward	Identify known data and find missing data, regardless of where it might appear in a problem Use inverse operations to work backward to find solutions

HOW DO WE GET THERE?

CCSS Practice Standard 1 provides us with a clear vision of the knowledge and skills that make our students effective problem solvers. But how do we help our students develop these important practices? Think about your own classroom as you read the following questions. You may already be able to answer "yes" to many of them!

What do we do each day in our classrooms to build mathematical thinkers?

▶ Do our classroom activities and discussions focus on students' thinking related to how and why they chose a particular strategy, rather than on just getting the answer?

▶ Do our classroom discussions move beyond oversimplified, and sometimes unreliable, methods like key words (e.g., "I saw the word *altogether* so I just added.")?

▶ Do we pose one or two problems for students to solve and discuss thoroughly, rather than supply a list of problems to be solved as quickly as possible?

▶ Do we often replace easier, more direct problems with problems that push students to apply their understanding of math content?

What do we do to keep our students actively engaged in solving problems?

▶ Do we routinely ask students to talk and write as they solve problems? Do we provide ongoing opportunities for them to talk about both process and solution, to identify their own thinking, and to discuss alternate ways to approach a problem?

▶ Are our questions frequent, purposeful, and high level?

▶ Do we maintain students' interest and expand their insights by asking them to share their ideas and actively solve problems with partners and groups?

How do we help our students develop positive attitudes and demonstrate perseverance during problem solving?

▶ Do we provide opportunities for students to explore complex problems that may include multiple approaches or answers that are not immediately apparent?

▶ Do we praise their efforts, with value placed on persistence and process rather than on the answer?

▸ Is our classroom environment supportive and nonthreatening? Is speed de-emphasized and is confusion openly discussed, including insights on ways to simplify problems and move through confusion?

▸ Do we acknowledge the efficiency of particular strategies but still celebrate individual, reasonable approaches?

What does problem solving look like and sound like? You probably see it more often in your students than you realize! As you read the classroom vignettes throughout this chapter and the rest of the book, think about when you've seen your own students using similar skills. In the pages that follow, we'll discuss ways you can help build students' proficiency with these math practices.

CLASSROOM-TESTED TECHNIQUES

Following are some valuable, classroom-tested techniques that work across grade levels and with varied math content to expand students' thinking and support the development of their problem-solving skills.

Focus on the Question

It can be daunting to think about the many skills we want to develop within our students and frustrating to think that each skill needs to be developed separately. Consider the following student expectations:

▸ Determine and articulate what the problem is asking

▸ Find a starting point by understanding mathematical situations

▸ Identify relevant data for solving the problem

▸ Identify an appropriate way to solve the problem

▸ Connect problem situations to abstract representations of the problem (e.g., equations, visuals) in order to clarify the task

▸ Identify or understand different ways to solve the problem

Focus on the Question is a simple classroom technique that addresses multiple problem-solving skills with little teacher planning, minimal class time, and no additional paperwork. In addition, it provides ongoing problem-solving experiences for students at all grade levels and can be easily integrated with various math content

Connections
to other practice standards

Students convert the problem situations to abstract equations in order to find solutions (Standard 2).

Students explain their choice of problem-solving strategies, construct viable arguments to justify their strategies, and precisely communicate their mathematical thinking (Standards 3 and 6).

(e.g., place value, fractions, measurement). This allows students to explore or review specific content skills through the problem situations. Here is how it works:

1. Post a set of data in the classroom on Monday (e.g., a picture graph of the colors of jellybeans in a bag, a list of the cost of snacks at a fair, a circle graph of favorite sports, or a list of the heights of students' bean plants in science). That data remains posted for the week.

2. Each day, pose a different problem in which students must use some or all of the data.

3. Each day, students talk to partners about what they are being asked to solve, what data will help them solve it, and how they would solve it.

4. Facilitate a class discussion in which students share their ideas about how the problem could be solved.

5. No answers are needed and written work is not required. The activity generally takes no more than 10 minutes.

In the Classroom

On Monday Mrs. Alexander posted the following situation and data on the board:

The Holiday Tree

The Partin family counted the different types of ornaments on the town's holiday tree. Here is the list of what they saw.

Stars – 24

Gingerbread men – 14

Snowflakes – 12

Reindeer – 18

Candy canes – 6

She asked her third-grade students to read the data with their partner, and then she posted the following problem:

> **Six of the reindeer had red noses. What fraction of the reindeer had red noses? Tell how you would get the answer.**

The students dove right into their discussions, talking about the question and debating how they would proceed to find the solution. They enthusiastically deliberated about the equation that might lead them to the answer, knowing that they did not have to find the actual answer. After several minutes, seeing that the students had discussed their plans of action, Mrs. Alexander asked them to share their thoughts with the class. She guided the discussion with questions that helped make their thinking visible to their classmates. The students, already having discussed their thinking with partners, were ready and willing to share their ideas.

Teacher: What is the question?

Liam: What fraction of reindeer ornaments had red noses?

Teacher: What does that mean? Can you say it another way?

Liam: Of all of the reindeer, what part had red noses?

Colin: It won't be a number. It will be a fraction.

Teacher: So, what data did you and your partner think might be important to solve the problem?

Molly: We need to know how many reindeer ornaments there are.

Teacher: Where would you find that data?

Molly: You just look at the list.

Blake: You use the number for the reindeer ornaments — 18.

Teacher: What about the rest of the data on the list? Do you need it?

Bailey: No.

Teacher: Why not?

Bailey: It just asked about reindeer ornaments, not the other ones.

Teacher: So we just ignore the other data?

Kate: Yes.

Allison: We don't need it.

Brendan: It doesn't matter for the problem.

Jason: But we also need to know 6 had red noses!

Teacher: I don't see that on the list.

Jason: No, it's in the problem.

Teacher: Oh, okay. So, what will you do with the data about the reindeer ornaments?

Patrick: We'll make a fraction with it.

Teacher: Why? Tell me what you mean.

Patrick: We know there were 6 reindeer with red noses and 18 altogether, so we make a fraction.

Kate: Yeah, so we know $\frac{6}{18}$ is the fraction.

Brendan: Yeah, $\frac{6}{18}$ have red noses.

Bailey: But you could say $\frac{1}{3}$.

Teacher: Could we say it that way?

Bailey: We could say both. They are the same thing.

Susan: Yeah, cause with fractions you can simplify them, but it means the same.

Patrick: Yeah, 6 + 6 + 6 = 18, so 6 is one out of three.

Susan: It would be the same answer, but $\frac{1}{3}$ sounds easier.

As the week unfolded, students explored a different problem each day using the same set of data about the holiday tree. Since an understanding of fractions was a primary expectation for her students, many of the problems required them to use their understanding of fractions as they contemplated a method to solve the problem. She posed questions like:

What fraction of the ornaments were snowflakes?

What fraction of the ornaments were edible?

If 6 of the stars were silver, what fraction of the stars were not silver?

Mrs. Alexander noticed a new level of confidence in her students as they talked about solving these problems. Early in the year, it had taken more prompting to get students to discuss their thinking, and she had felt many moments of awkward silence as they considered her questions. Now, after many experiences with these types of discussions, they were relaxing, more easily identifying the question and the data that would help them solve it, and they appeared comfortable debating their decisions about ways to solve the problem.

By using the same data each day, but changing the question, students become skilled at pinpointing the question and identifying the specific data needed for that particular question. The data that is used one day is not the same data that is used on the following day. In the same way, the equation that solves the problem on Monday is different from the one that solves Tuesday's problem. Students begin to see that the question guides them to the relevant data and the appropriate strategy.

The key to effectively implementing this technique is the questions we pose during the class discussions. Asking open-ended questions, such as the ones in Figure 2.2, makes our students' thinking visible. Those students who struggle with problem solving hear how others approach problem tasks. Students hear alternate

Figure 2.2 *These questions prompt students to communicate about their thinking.*

QUESTIONS TO GUIDE STUDENT THINKING

▶ What is the question?

  ▸ Can you restate it in your own words?
  ▸ Can anyone say it a different way?

▶ What information will you need to solve it?

  ▸ Where will you find the information?
  ▸ Do you need all of the information on the list, table, graph, etc.? Why or why not?
  ▸ How did you know which information is needed?

▶ What should you do with the information?

  ▸ Should you add, subtract, multiply, or divide? Which one? Why?
  ▸ What in the problem tells you to add, subtract, multiply, or divide?
  ▸ What is the equation that matches this problem?

▶ Is there another way to solve it?

  ▸ Could you have used a different operation? Explain which one and why.
  ▸ Could you have made a diagram or used manipulatives to solve it? Explain how.
  ▸ How are these different ways connected?

Later, we will explore modeling as a critical math practice (Standard 4). Notice how modeling is integrated into this problem-solving experience.

strategies chosen by their classmates and expand their repertoire of approaches. The activity also allows students to revisit various types of graphs and math concepts throughout the year and discuss solutions to many different types of math problems. In addition, students gain confidence and increase their skills in reading and analyzing word problems through ongoing modeling and think-alouds related to analyzing details, making inferences, and other comprehension skills.

Whether you use this activity with a small group of students or the whole class, you will enjoy the conversations that emerge during *Focus on the Question*, and these conversations will not only guide your students' thinking but will also provide you with a wealth of information about the current level of their problem-solving skills.

Give It a Try!

Below you will find three examples of *Focus on the Question* at three different levels (primary, intermediate, and middle grades), including a data set and five questions related to the data. Keep in mind that it is the questions you ask that get your students thinking and talking about their problem-solving efforts.

Primary Example

Gathering Seashells

The children were picking up seashells at the beach.

The graph shows the number of shells that each child picked up.

OUR SHELLS	1	2	3	4	5	6	7	8	9
Katie	▓	▓	▓	▓					
Bridget	▓	▓	▓						
Jackie	▓	▓	▓	▓	▓	▓	▓	▓	▓
Allison	▓	▓	▓	▓	▓	▓	▓		
Kim	▓	▓	▓	▓					

Number of Shells

Day 1   Katie and Kim put their shells in a box. How many did they have altogether? Tell how you would find the answer.

Day 2   Allison wanted to collect 10 shells. How many more will she need to collect? Tell how you would find the answer.

Day 3   Jackie wanted to collect a dozen shells. How many more does she have to collect to have a dozen? Tell how you would find the answer.

Day 4   Allison said she collected more shells by herself than Katie and Kim collected together. Is she right? Tell how you would find the answer.

Day 5   How many shells did the children collect altogether? Tell how you know.

Intermediate Example

Shipley Aquarium

Admission Cost

Adults – $8.00

Children (ages 3 and over) – $6.50

Children (ages 2 and under) – Free

Day 1   How much more does an adult pay to get into the aquarium than a six-year-old child? Tell how you would get the answer.

Day 2   Mr. and Mrs. Jones brought their two-year-old son to the aquarium. How much did they pay for admission? Tell how you would get the answer.

Day 3   Karen had her 10th birthday party at the aquarium. She invited 6 friends. What was the total admission cost for the seven children? Tell how you would get the answer.

Day 4   The third grade took a field trip to the aquarium. There were 20 children and 3 adults. How much was admission? Tell how you would get the answer.

Day 5   Some adults went to the aquarium. They paid $48.00 for admission. How many adults were there? Tell how you would get the answer.

Middle Grades Example

There were 420 students who ate lunch in the cafeteria. Following are their lunch choices.

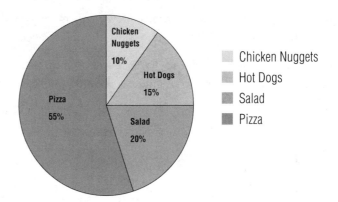

Day 1   Each plate of chicken nuggets was served with three carrot sticks. How many carrot sticks were needed? Tell how you would get the answer.

Day 2   How many more students ordered salad than hot dogs? Tell how you would get the answer.

Day 3   One-third of the pizza orders were for pepperoni pizza and $\frac{2}{3}$ were for sausage pizza. How many orders were for each kind? Tell how you would get the answer.

Day 4   Two-thirds of the students who ordered a hot dog took a ketchup packet, $\frac{1}{7}$ took a mustard packet, and the rest took one of each. How many ketchup packets and how many mustard packets were taken that day? Tell how you would get the answer.

Day 5   The cafeteria orders packages of lettuce to make the salads. Each package holds 2 pounds of lettuce. Each salad was made with approximately 10 ounces of lettuce. How many packages did they need? Tell how you got your answer.

Posing Open-Ended Questions

The questions we ask during math class have so much power! We can ask questions that stifle learning by prompting a quick number response. We know these questions all too well from our own experiences.

What is the answer to number 3 on your worksheet?

How many degrees are in a right angle?

What is 4 × 5?

How many feet are in a yard?

We recognize that these questions do not require mathematical thinking, do not create proficient mathematicians, and do not promote the Practices we are focusing on in the CCSS Practice Standards. We have the power to select questions that build proficient mathematicians.

As we explore questioning, we recognize two distinct opportunities within our classrooms: posing rich problems for students to solve and posing thoughtful, open-ended questions as students explore mathematical ideas.

POSING RICH MATH PROBLEMS   Rich problems are those that require students to think beyond a quick response. These problems promote discussion, thinking, and perseverance (see Figure 2.3). They may be able to be solved in multiple ways and may even have multiple solutions. Consider the modifications to the problems in Figure 2.4. The modified problems require more thinking, can be solved in a variety of ways, and may lead to varied solutions. Ongoing experience with these types of problems, along with a supportive classroom environment, helps build students' perseverance as it shows that quick answers are often not possible and that a bit of a struggle is a natural part of math problem solving.

Connections
to other practice standards

Rich math problems require students to construct viable arguments as they explain their responses (Standard 3).

Students model with mathematics as they explain and justify their solutions to open-ended questions or tasks (Standard 4).

Figure 2.3 *Students benefit from opportunities to work with partners to discuss rich problems.*

Figure 2.4 *Creating problems with more complexity challenges students to apply their mathematical thinking.*

TRADITIONAL PROBLEM	RICH PROBLEM
What is 6 + 4?	Ten children went to the movie. How many were girls? How many were boys? Explain your answer. Could there be other answers?
Molly has a quarter, 2 nickels, and a dime. How much money does she have?	Molly has 6 coins in her piggy bank. She has more than 85¢, but less than $1.10. What coins could she have? Explain your answers.
Three children shared a pizza. They each had the same amount. What fraction did each child have?	Three children are sharing a pizza. How might they share it? What fraction of the pizza could each child get? Justify your answers.
A rectangle has a length of 4 units and a width of 3 units. What is the area?	Create rectangles with an area of 24 square units. How are they alike and different? Are their perimeters the same? Explain your observations.
How many hours of TV do you watch in a week?	How many hours (or years) of TV would you have watched if you live to be 100 years old? Be ready to justify your answer.
What is the surface area of a box that is 8 inches tall, 6 inches wide, and 12 inches long?	(Provide students with several boxes and a roll of gift wrap with dimensions on the label.) How many rolls of gift wrap will be needed to cover all of the boxes? Justify your answer.

Connections
to other practice standards

Deep questions require students to construct viable arguments as they explain their thinking (Standard 3).

Deep questions challenge students to look for patterns or generalizations (Standards 7 and 8).

Rich tasks require our students to think and act like mathematicians. See Appendix D for sample rich tasks at primary, intermediate, and middle grades levels. (The tasks are also available at www.heinemann.com/putting-the-practices-into-action). These tasks challenge our students to use multiple math practices.

REFINING OUR GUIDING QUESTIONS   At all grade levels, teacher questioning is a critical component of problem-solving instruction. Mrs. King's first-grade class gathered data and created a picture graph about their pets. The graph included dogs, cats, birds, and fish. Mrs. King paired the students and posed the following problem:

> *How many of our pets have four legs?*

1.OA.1

Note that, rather than asking students to find the number of cats and dogs, she asked for the number of four-legged animals. This simple change in questioning required her primary students to employ reasoning skills to determine the appropriate data.

Mrs. King reminded her students that they would be sharing their ideas and that they should be ready to show how they had figured out the solution. She encouraged them to solve the problem in a way that made sense to them. The students worked with their partners, discussing the numbers of legs on various animals, reasoning about which data to use, and deciding how to approach the problem. Some students immediately grabbed counters to represent the animals, others grabbed paper and a pencil to record ideas with either numbers or pictures. Some used addition and created a number sentence to represent the total number of cats and dogs. After the students had explored the problem, Mrs. King began a sharing circle. Partners shared their work and Mrs. King probed with questions to make their thinking visible. She purposefully solicited ideas from partners who had solved the problem in different ways, wanting to highlight their different approaches.

> The expectation is for more than an answer. Students are asked to explain how they got their answer. This shifts the focus from the answer to the process.

Teacher: How did you know which animals to count?

Emma: They needed 4 legs.

Teacher: Kristen and John, why didn't you use the data about fish or birds?

Kristen: Birds have 2 legs.

John: Fish don't have any legs!

Teacher: But they were on the graph, shouldn't we use them?

Kristen: No! They don't have 4 legs.

Teacher: Oscar and Deryn, why did you use counters?

Oscar: They were the cats and dogs.

Deryn: We put one for each cat and dog.

Teacher: After you used counters to show the number of cats and dogs, how did you get your answer?

Oscar: We counted all of the counters.

Deryn: We had to count them all 'cause they all had 4 legs. We started with the 5 dogs and then we counted on for the cats: 6, 7, 8, 9. (as she demonstrated her counting by pointing to each counter)

Teacher: Molly and Blake added. Why did you add?

Blake: We added 'cause we put them together. Adding is counting all of them.

Molly: We joined them together. That's what you do when you add.

Teacher: Why did you write 4 + 5?

Molly: There were 4 cats and 5 dogs and they all have 4 legs, so we knew it was 4 + 5.

Aidan: You could count too if you wanted.

Teacher: Would you get the same answer?

Aidan: Yes!

Madison: We all got the same even if we drew it.

Jordan: Counting and adding give you the same. It's the same. (she counted the marks on her diagram to show 9)

The students showed multiple ways to solve the problem, from drawing pictures to using counters to creating number sentences. They proudly talked about their mathematical thinking and were interested to see the various ways their classmates found the total number of four-legged animals.

Regardless of grade level, providing opportunities for partner and group discussions during problem solving allows students to investigate strategies together. Asking students to share two ways to solve a problem can stretch their thinking. Orchestrating a class sharing time, in which students show and talk about how they solved problems, allows them to pause and reflect on how and why they did what they did.

--- **Give It a Try!** ---

The questions in Figure 2.5 are particularly helpful as we focus on the development of problem-solving skills. Frequently asking our students to articulate, both orally and in writing, how they solved problems and why they chose their strategies is an

Figure 2.5 *These questions guide our students' thinking as they solve math problems.*

OPEN-ENDED QUESTIONS TO PROMOTE PROBLEM SOLVING

▶ Before

  ▶ What is the question?

  ▶ What data will help you find the solution?

  ▶ How will you get started solving this problem?

  ▶ Does this problem remind you of any others you have solved?

  ▶ What did you do to solve that problem? Will it work here?

▶ During

  ▶ Are you blocked? Should you try a new approach?

  ▶ Does your answer make sense? Why or why not? If it doesn't make sense, what could you do?

▶ After

  ▶ How did you solve the problem?

  ▶ Why did you solve the problem that way?

  ▶ What was easy/hard about solving this problem?

  ▶ Where did you get stuck? How did you get unstuck?

  ▶ Were you confused at any point? How did you simplify the task or clarify the problem?

  ▶ Can you describe another way to solve the problem? Which way might be more efficient?

  ▶ Is there another answer? Explain.

important part of problem-solving instruction. Our goal is for students to self-regulate their thinking, not needing as much support from us, so prompting should decrease as students become more adept at solving problems. See Appendix B for a convenient bookmark of these questions. Place it in your teacher's guide, on your desk, or by your daily lesson plans to guide you during your classroom questioning.

ADDITIONAL IDEAS FOR DEVELOPING THE PRACTICE

The chart in Figure 2.6 shares effective Student Practices related to Practice Standard 1 and offers suggestions for ways you might develop these Practices. This is not intended to be a checklist in which you attempt to complete each item on the list, but rather suggestions for teaching options that address essential Student Practices.

Figure 2.6 *This chart provides suggestions for ways a teacher might address specific problem-solving skills.*

Our students are better able to . . .	Because as teachers we . . .
Determine and articulate what the problem is asking.	Ask students to restate the problem in their own words. Have students turn to a partner to state the problem.
Find a starting point by understanding mathematical situations.	Use diagrams to model math situations. Frequently ask, "What should we do first?" or "How should we get started?"
Identify an appropriate way to solve the problem.	Discuss familiar problems (When have we seen something like this before? What did we do?). Discuss the efficiency of various strategies (Will it work? Why does the strategy make sense with this problem? Which strategy is more efficient?).
Connect problem situations to abstract representations of the problem (e.g., equations, visuals) in order to clarify the task.	Avoid simply circling key words to decide on the appropriate operation and instead focus on identifying the concepts or actions of the operations (i.e., Why should we add to solve this problem? What is the problem asking us to do? Why add, subtract, multiply, or divide?). Consistently discuss building appropriate equations to solve problems (What equation shows this situation?). Provide materials (e.g., manipulatives, paper/pencil) to allow students to visualize situations.
Self-monitor their progress and change directions when necessary; adjust strategies when having difficulty.	Think aloud to show students how we change course when needed during the problem-solving process. Have students talk or write about how they got stuck and then unstuck when solving a problem.
Demonstrate perseverance and make adjustments until a problem is solved.	Think aloud, acknowledging that everyone feels like giving up at times. Share ways we persevere or demonstrate patience when solving problems (e.g., "I'm getting frustrated. Let me try something else . . ."). Ask questions like, "Are you getting stuck? What else could you do?" Acknowledge those who modify their thinking and persevere to get to the solution rather than acknowledging the quickest to get to the answer.

Figure 2.6 *Continued*

Our students are better able to . . .	Because as teachers we . . .
Articulate the strategies they use to solve problems.	Provide opportunities for partner and group discussions while solving problems.
	Frequently ask students to articulate, both orally and in writing, how they solved problems and why they chose their strategy.
	Orchestrate a class sharing time so students can show and talk about how they solved problems.
Identify or understand different ways to solve a problem.	Make classroom lists of possible strategies.
	Share alternate strategies when discussing how a problem was solved.
	Encourage students to show two ways to solve a problem.
Articulate the reasonableness of strategies or solutions.	Frequently ask, "Does your answer make sense? Why?"
	Ask students to predict/estimate prior to computing the solution to a problem, and then compare their answer to their estimate to check for reasonableness.
	Ask students to go back to the question and restate the question followed by their answer. Does the answer work with the question?

ASSESSMENT TIP

PUT IT IN WRITING

Asking students to write about how they solve problems, why they choose a particular strategy, how they adjust their thinking during the problem-solving process, and what is easy or hard about the task all promote reflection and allow us to assess our students' problem-solving skills. The student in Figure 2.7 explains his approach to a problem, including the way he adjusted his approach after finding that his first strategy (folding the paper and simply counting the folds) was not going to work. By gathering some data and organizing it in a table, he was able to see and extend a pattern to find the solution.

Figure 2.7   *This student's writing shows his thinking as he solved the problem and highlights his perseverance as he adjusted his strategy when his first attempt was ineffective.*

> Jim folded a piece of paper in half 8 times. How many sections were there when he unfolded it?
>
> Tell how you found your answer.
>
> there will be 256 sections. I started to fold paper but there were to many to count, so I made a table. I saw that the number of sections doubled each time
>
> | folds | 1 | 2 | 3 | 4 | 5 | 6 | 7 | 8 |
> |---|---|---|---|---|---|---|---|---|
> | Sections | 2 | 4 | 8 | 16 | 32 | 64 | 128 | 256 |

Some key writing prompts include:

- How did you solve this problem?
- What strategy did you choose? Why?
- Was there another way to solve the problem? Explain.
- Did you get stuck at any point in this problem? How did you get unstuck?
- What was easy about solving this problem? What was hard?
- Did this problem remind you of any others you have solved? In what ways?

SUMMING IT UP

Teaching problem solving is more than assigning problems to our students. It is a balance of guided experiences in which we support the development of our students' thinking skills, as well as investigative experiences in which our students develop skills through trial-and-error experiences.

Did you recognize some of your own students in the vignettes? Did you see some of your own teaching practices in the suggestions throughout the chapter? Consider the following as you reflect on strengthening your students' problem-solving experiences:

Do I routinely provide opportunities for my students to share their solutions and processes with partners, groups, and the whole class?

Do I show my students that I value process (how they did it) rather than simply the correct answer?

Do I pose problems that require perseverance? Do I use thoughtful questions to guide and encourage students as they struggle with problems?

We have come a long way in our understanding of the teaching of problem solving. We want to recognize and celebrate our successes as we continue to refine our teaching.

Exploring Standard 2:
Reason Abstractly and Quantitatively

Although each chapter in this book addresses a specific CCSS Standard for Mathematical Practice, these standards are most definitely interwoven. As you read each chapter, notice the connection between the Practice Standard addressed within that chapter and those that have been discussed previously. Keep in mind that these standards show the Practices of effective mathematicians, and those Practices cannot be isolated into specific categories.

WHY QUANTITATIVE AND ABSTRACT REASONING?

Quantitative reasoning is the ability to apply math skills and concepts to solve real problems. In our everyday lives, we are challenged to read and use quantitative data and apply quantitative skills to solve real problems. Whether we are analyzing advertisements, making financial decisions, or simply understanding the things we read in a newspaper, we must go beyond our ability to compute. Our need to interpret data and judge their accuracy is undeniable. Everyone should possess the skills to understand and use quantitative concepts.

It would be impossible to memorize how to solve every math problem. In order to solve problems, we employ *abstract reasoning* skills. We change real situations to abstractions (e.g., equations, variables, and expressions). If we understand those abstractions and what they represent, we can accurately manipulate them to find solutions. Abstract reasoning is necessary to solve math problems.

UNDERSTANDING THE STANDARD

This standard addresses the importance of building a strong understanding of numbers (quantities). When faced with a math problem, students must be able to represent the problem using abstractions (e.g., numbers, symbols, and diagrams). Students must see the connection between the problem situation and the abstract representation (equation) that stands for the problem.

Mathematically proficient students are able to:

▶ represent quantities in a variety of ways

▶ remove the problem context to solve the problem in an abstract way (equation)

▶ refer back to the problem context, when needed, to understand and evaluate the answer.

Putting It in the Abstract

Mathematically proficient students understand problems and the quantities in those problems. They are able to convert a problem to an abstract representation using numbers, symbols, equations, diagrams, or manipulatives. Consider the following examples in which students share their varied representations of a problem. These students understand quantities, are able to determine when to use certain operations (add or multiply) or approaches (count or diagram), and can construct equations or other representations that match the problems.

Example A

> *Lisa had 6 pretzels. She ate 4. How many did she have left?*

K.OA.2; 1.OA.1

Colleen represented the problem with an equation:

$6 - 4 = n$

(If 4 pretzels were taken from the original 6 pretzels, how many remained?)

Mike chose to represent the same problem with a different, but appropriate, equation:

$$4 + n = 6$$

(The 4 pretzels she ate and the ones she had left total 6 pretzels.)

Megan drew a diagram to represent the problem:

Betsy used 6 counters to show her understanding of the problem, removing 4 counters from the original 6 and then counting the number of counters left.

Example B

There were 9 cupcakes on the plate. Three of them were chocolate and the rest were vanilla. What fraction of the cupcakes were vanilla?

3.NF.1

Clare used 9 two-color counters to represent the problem. She turned 3 of them to the red side to show the chocolate cupcakes and left the remaining counters on the yellow side (vanilla) and showed her solution as $\frac{6}{9}$. She shared that 6 of the 9 total cupcakes were vanilla.

Danny drew a 3 × 3 array with 9 circles. He circled 3 of them and counted the rest. He showed his solution as $\frac{6}{9}$.

Maddy also drew a 3 × 3 array with 9 circles. She circled two columns of 3 and showed her solution as $\frac{2}{3}$.

Megan simply said that the fraction that was vanilla was $\frac{6}{9}$ because 6 cupcakes were vanilla (since 3 were chocolate) and there were 9 total cupcakes on the plate.

> Notice the ways in which students are modeling the problems. Modeling is Practice Standard 4 and will be addressed in depth in Chapter 5.

Example C

Joe watched TV for 90 minutes each day, seven days a week. How many hours of TV did he watch in 3 weeks?

4.MD.2

Kevin created the equation $(1.5 \times 7) \times 3 = n$. One and a half hours each day for 7 days represents how many hours he watched TV each week. His weekly total multiplied by 3 shows the total hours in 3 weeks.

Rita decided to represent the problem with the equation $1.5 \times 21 = n$ since Joe watched TV every day for 3 weeks, which is 21 days. $1\frac{1}{2}$ hours each day multiplied by 21 days gives the total hours of TV he watched for 3 weeks.

Students who understand operations and quantities are able to represent problems in a variety of ways.

Contextualize and Decontextualize

Numbers and symbols stand for something. Recognizing this, and knowing what each stands for in any given situation, is an essential part of being a successful mathematician. In order to successfully interpret and solve math problems, students need to be able to decontextualize and contextualize problems. The following examples explain these mathematical terms:

> *100 students and 5 chaperones went on the field trip. Each bus held 35 people. How many buses were needed?*

Kathy *decontextualizes* the problem by replacing the context with numbers and symbols (creating an abstraction of the problem). She determines that there are 105 people who will need to ride the buses and 35 people can ride on each bus. If she is splitting 105 people into groups of 35, she realizes that she will be dividing and builds the equation $105 \div 35 = n$. Then she solves it: $105 \div 35 = 3$. But to truly solve the problem, Kathy needs to understand what the 3 means. To do that, she *recontextualizes* it—she refers back to the context of the problem to understand that the 3 means 3 buses.

But consider the following problem:

> *120 students and 5 chaperones went on the field trip. Each bus held 35 people. How many buses were needed?*

Dan *decontextualizes* the problem as he considers the data and the action of the problem (dividing the people into groups of 35) and creates the equation $125 \div 35 = n$ to represent the problem in an abstract way. He solves the equation and gets $125 \div 35 = 3.5714$. But does this answer make sense? In abstract numbers and symbols it makes perfect sense, but as Dan refers back to the context of buses it makes no sense. There cannot be 3.5714 buses. Dan has to *recontextualize* the answer by referring back to the problem and realizes that he needs a whole number of buses. Three buses would be too few, so the answer must be 4 buses.

Understanding the units and quantities within a problem is an important factor in making sense of the numbers within the problem. While students often convert the problem to an equation and then work with the data in an abstract way, labeling answers forces students to refer back to the context of the problem. What is the answer when solving 2.5×3? 7.5 dogs is not possible, 7.5 inches is $7\frac{1}{2}$ inches, 7.5 dozen is 7 dozen plus 6 more, 7.5 feet is 7 feet and 6 inches, 7.5 cupcakes is

> Labeling answers provides formative assessment data. The numeric part of the answer will attest to students' computational accuracy, while the label will attest to whether the student knows what that quantity represents.

7 cupcakes plus $\frac{1}{2}$ a cupcake. The meaning of 7.5—and the ultimate answer to the problem—varies with the context.

HOW DO WE GET THERE?

CLASSROOM-TESTED TECHNIQUES

So how do we help our students develop these important Practices? Following are some valuable, classroom-tested techniques that work across grade levels and with varied math content to strengthen students' ability to represent problems in abstract ways (equations, expressions, inequalities) and to see the connection between equations and real situations.

NUMBER WEBS   Number webs encourage flexibility with numbers. Students are given a quantity and asked to express that quantity in as many ways as possible. The number 25 might be expressed as $20 + 5$; $100 - 75$; 2 tens and 5 ones; 5×5; the amount of pennies in a quarter; $(2 \times 10) + 5$, and more. Students might write a word problem that results in 25. Number webs are effective at all levels, with the data becoming more complex as fractions, decimals, percents, exponents, and variables are introduced (see Figure 3.1). Primary students might be asked to web 5, while

Connections
to other practice standards

Students find precise combinations of numbers equivalent to the target number (Standard 6).

Students may identify patterns in expressions equivalent to the target number (e.g., when creating addition expressions, students may observe that increasing an addend by one lessens the other addend by 1 (Standard 7).

Students developing computational fluency may need tools such as hundred charts or number lines to aid in their precision (Standard 5).

Figure 3.1   *This number web shows the students' understanding of the various ways that 1.25 can be represented.*

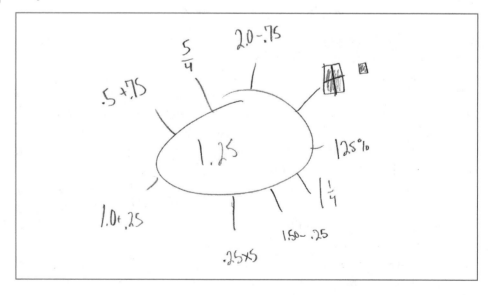

intermediate students web $\frac{3}{4}$, and middle grades students web 8^3. Students might work with partners to create their webs and then share their representations of the number with the larger group in order to expand their classmates' thinking about the selected quantity.

FOCUS ON THE QUESTION   We discussed *Focus on the Question* in Chapter 2 because of its emphasis on the problem-solving process. This technique also provides tremendous support as students strengthen their abilities to represent problems with equations. Each day, as a new problem is posed, students must decide how to create an equation that accurately represents that day's situation. Many of the classroom activities presented throughout this book work to support students' skills with multiple math practices.

> **Connections**
> **to other practice standards**
>
> Writing problems to contextualize mathematics aids students' ability to solve problems as they strengthen their understanding of the link between real situations and math equations (Standard 1).

HEADLINE STORIES   You can get an idea of what a newspaper story will be about just by reading the headline. In just a few words, the headline sums up the story. An equation is like a newspaper headline—short and to the point. In the same way that a headline is connected to a story, an equation is connected to a word problem. Students can be asked to write stories to go along with math headlines (equations). The equation sums up the story (word problem). Here is an example of a headline and a word problem that goes along with it.

> **headline: 3 × 4 = 12**

> **3.OA.1**

One student might write, "Julie had 3 sheets of stickers. Each sheet had 4 stickers on it. How many stickers did she have?" Another student might produce, "There were 3 nests with 4 eggs in each one. How many eggs were there?" There are many other stories that might go with the same equation. Students might be asked to write problems about equations or inequalities that might contain whole numbers, variables, fractions, decimals, or percents.

Headline Stories can be as easy or as difficult as you make them and still allow you to assess students' understanding of abstractions. Fifth-grade students were given the equation $5 \times 1.5 = n$ and asked to solve for n. They needed to write a problem to show that they understood what 5×1.5 might represent. In Figure 3.2, the student accurately describes a situation that matches 5×1.5, with 5 being the number of pets and 1.5 being the quantity of food each pet receives (1.5 cups). The operation of multiplication makes sense with this story, since n is the total amount of food needed to feed all of the pets.

> **5.NBT.1; 5.NBT.7**

Figure 3.2 *This student created a problem that shows an understanding of the equation 5 × 1.5 = n.*

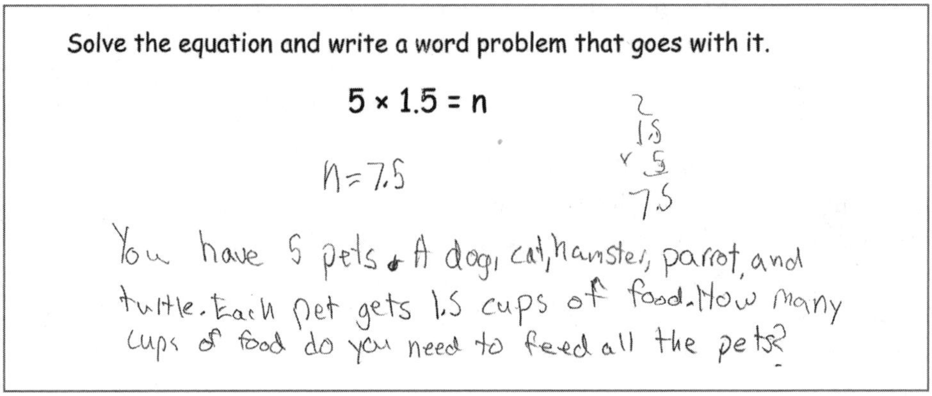

> **Solve the equation and write a word problem that goes with it.**
>
> $$5 \times 1.5 = n$$
>
> n = 7.5
>
> 2
> 1.5
> × 5
> 7.5
>
> You have 5 pets. A dog, cat, hamster, parrot, and turtle. Each pet gets 1.5 cups of food. How many cups of food do you need to feed all the pets?

We often assume that our students have a solid understanding of math operations and can move easily from real situations to abstract representations of those situations. Posing *Headline Stories* can be an eye-opening experience. We see our students' understandings and misunderstandings. In Figure 3.3, the student's word problem does not match the equation. This student is not demonstrating an understanding of the concept of multiplication or an understanding of what each quantity represents. This student would benefit from working with a partner to construct problems related to multiplication equations, drawing pictures or using manipulatives to represent multiplication equations, or participation in a small teacher-led group with further discussions and modeling related to the concept of multiplication.

Figure 3.3 *This student's story does not make sense with the equation. A basic misunderstanding related to multiplication is evident.*

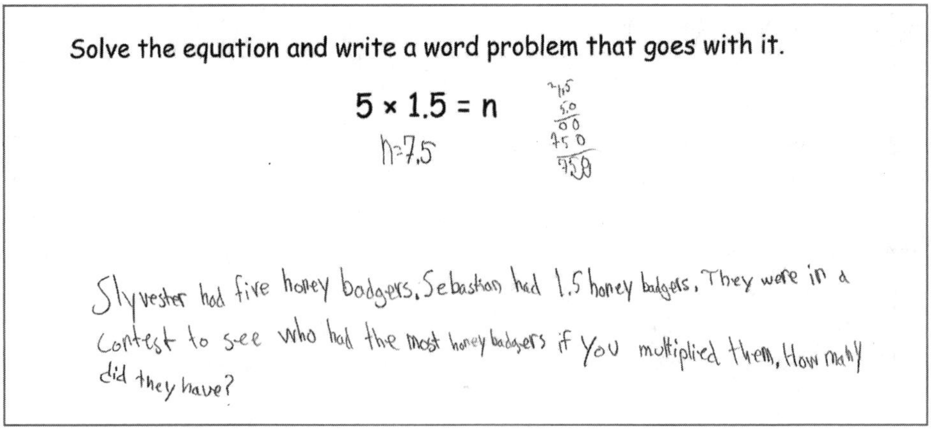

> **Solve the equation and write a word problem that goes with it.**
>
> $$5 \times 1.5 = n$$
>
> n=7.5
>
> 1.5
> 5.0
> 0 0
> 75 0
> 750
>
> Slyvester had five honey badgers. Sebastion had 1.5 honey badgers. They were in a contest to see who had the most honey badgers. If you multiplied them, How many did they have?

Other students in the fifth-grade class wrote the following problems for $5 \times 1.5 = n$. Carmen wrote:

Jake is at the store and needs 5 pounds of rice. One pound of rice costs $1.50. How much money will Jake have to spend for 5 pounds of rice?

Carmen demonstrated her understanding of $5 \times 1.5 = n$ with an appropriate problem.

Allison wrote:

Emily and her friends are going on a picnic. She is going to give each one of her friends 1.5 apples. There are 5 people going including her. How many apples is Emily going to need in total?

While Allison is able to write an equation that works mathematically, it might be helpful to discuss real situations that make sense. Is 1.5 apples a typical snack? Would a different item make more sense with the quantities in this equation?

Steven wrote:

You have 5 slices of pizza. Then your mom multiplies your amount of slices of pizza by 1.5. How much slices of pizza do you have now?

Clearly, Steven gave up and decided to have Mom mandate the multiplication. He may be confused about the concept of multiplication, or he may be having difficulty working with the decimal in the equation. Including Steven in a small group to determine the reasons for his confusion would be indicated.

Angela wrote:

Jane and Katy had 1.5 chocolate chip cookies. They had 5 empty containers. Jane and Katy wanted to divide the cookies so that there would be an equal amount of cookie in each container. $5 \times 1.5 = 7.5$ Each container contained 7.5 pieces of cookie.

There is a lot of confusion in Angela's problem. She is forcing the equation into the story. Why are we dividing the cookies into pieces? How does this relate to multiplication? Could we diagram this or act it out to see if it shows the operation of multiplication? Thinking aloud while developing a class, or small-group, problem might help Angela see the multiplicative thinking more clearly.

Young students may begin the process of abstraction through pictures, such as the student in Figure 3.4. This student recognized that combining 6 lollipops and 4 lollipops could be a context for $6 + 4 = 10$. The student in Figure 3.5 has gained the skills to write the story, still accurately finding a context for $6 + 4 = 10$.

K.OA.2; 1.OA.1

Figure 3.4   *This student decides on the context of two sets of lollipops to appropriately show* 6 + 4 = 10.

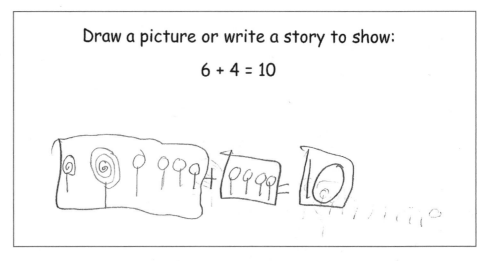

Draw a picture or write a story to show:

6 + 4 = 10

Figure 3.5   *This student writes: "Once there was 6 sheep in a barn. They saw 4 more sheep in the barn. Then the farmer came out. He counted the sheep. He counted 6 and 4 and he had 10." This student understands the operation of addition and is able to contextualize* 6 + 4.

Draw a picture or write a story to show:

6 + 4 = 10

Onece there was 6 sheep in a baren. They sol 4 more sheep in the baren. Then the faremer came out he cawted the sheep. He cawted 6 and 4 and he had 10.

Give It a Try!

Allow students to work with groups or partners to write problems to match equations. Have students talk about the equation together to generate ideas (i.e., What could the topic be? What will the data represent? What could happen in their story that matches this equation?). Have students write the problem and the equation on their paper and then share the various problems with the class.

Some variations you might try:

▶ *Post It:* Create a class bulletin board displaying varied problems that go with the same equation.

▶ *Book It:* Create a class book with each page containing a different story about the equation.

▶ *Reverse It:* Present students with a word problem. Ask them to write the equation that matches the word problem. Have them tell you what each number in their equation represents.

▶ *Match It:* Provide students with 2 sets of index cards—one set containing different equations (one on each card), the other set containing corresponding problems (these could be student-written problems from the previous day). Have students work with partners to match each equation to the corresponding problem. Ask them to justify their matches.

▶ *Question It:* Tell the answer. Ask students to write the question (in the form of a word problem).

Answer = 10   The problem is . . .

Answer = $3\frac{1}{2}$ The problem is . . .

Answer = $4.50   The problem is . . .

Answer = 40%   The problem is . . .

ADDITIONAL IDEAS FOR DEVELOPING THE PRACTICE

How do we help our students deepen their understanding of numbers, contextualize and decontextualize as they solve problems, and better understand quantities? Consider the following ideas. Which do you already do? Which might help to strengthen your students' skills?

Our students are better able to . . .	Because as teachers we . . .
Make sense of quantities and their relationships in problem situations.	Ask students to identify and describe the data in the problem. Ask students to build equations to represent problems.
Decontextualize.	Discuss selecting appropriate operations to solve problems (e.g., Would it make sense to add, subtract, multiply, or divide?). Model building appropriate equations to solve problems. Use diagrams to model math situations to make it easier to see what is happening in the problems. Can students draw a diagram to show a word problem for 3 × 5? Frequently ask, "What operation makes sense?" or "How should we build an equation to match this problem?"
Contextualize.	Ask students to write a word problem to go with a given equation (see *Headline Stories*). Consistently ask students to explain equations or diagrams, connecting them to the problem scenario (e.g., What does the 6 represent in our equation 6 × 3 = 18?). Ask students to label answers by referring back to the problem to determine what the quantity (solution) represents. Ask students if the quantity makes sense when referring back to the problem (e.g., Does 3.5714 buses make sense?).
Know and flexibly use different properties of numbers.	Model and discuss flexible use of numbers. Discuss building appropriate equations to solve problems (i.e., What equation shows this situation? Is there more than one equation that would represent the problem? Would properties like commutative, associative, or distributive allow you to create different equations for the same problem?).

ASSESSMENT TIP

Pinch cards (O'Connell 2007a) provide focused instruction to build students' skills at creating appropriate equations to solve problems, but they are also a strong formative assessment tool. Each card is made from an index card, with the operation signs printed in the same location on the front and back of the card (see Figure 3.6). (You can find sample pinch cards at www. heinemann.com/putting-the-practices-into-action.)

Figure 3.6 *Pinch cards allow teachers to quickly see the operation each student selects.*

1. Give each student a pinch card and pose a math problem, asking students to indicate the operation they would use to solve the problem by silently pinching the sign on their card. For multistep problems, students might pinch two operations. Through a quick scan of the room, you can see the operations selected by each student and can quickly assess their understanding. (Is this problem difficult for all students? Are there a few students who might benefit from small-group assistance?)

2. Ask students to turn to partners and share the operation(s) they believe would solve the problem and justify why they chose that operation. Move around the room, listening to students' comments.

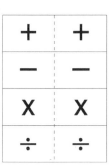

3. Facilitate a class discussion in which students share their operations and justifications, with you prompting, as necessary, for detailed reasoning. Have the class work together to build the appropriate equation(s) as you record their suggestions on the board.

In this activity all students are engaged, share their reasoning, and are involved in the construction of the equations. You can pose and discuss one problem, or pose and discuss a few, dependent on the time available. Using the pinch cards and listening to students' discussions with partners, you are able to quickly spot misunderstandings or confusions and immediately address them during the class discussions.

Dependent on the grade level, you might use problems like the following:

▶ There were 3 white dogs and 4 brown dogs. How many dogs were there?

▶ Jenny had 10 pennies in her pocket. One fell out. How many pennies were left in her pocket?

▶ Colleen loves playing basketball. Her team has played four games so far this year. She scored 11 points in the first game, 14 points in the second game, 16 points in the third game, and 12 points in the fourth game. How many points has she scored so far this season?

- There were 6 soccer teams in the league and 12 players on each team. How many players were in the league?

- Katie's mom baked 24 cookies. Katie and her 5 friends shared them. Each person got the same number of cookies. How many cookies did each person get?

- A package of hot dogs cost $2.50 and a bag of potato chips cost $1.79. Rita bought one package of hot dogs and 2 bags of potato chips for the cookout. How much did it cost? (Note that students can pinch two operations if they feel that two operations are needed to solve the problem.)

- Manny ate $\frac{1}{2}$ of the pizza and Jilly ate $\frac{1}{3}$. How much of the pizza did they eat?

- The 4 members of the High Rollers Bowling Team scored 120, 136, 128, and 162. What was the team's mean score?

SUMMING IT UP

Mathematicians represent situations with numbers and symbols. To be mathematically proficient, our students must recognize the connection between a problem and an abstract representation of that problem (e.g., an equation, expression, or inequality). The ability to decontextualize a problem, and then contextualize as needed when solving the problem, are essential problem-solving skills. The ability to recognize varied ways to represent quantities strengthens students' skills, as does the ability to analyze solutions by considering the context of a problem.

Exploring Standard 3:
Construct Viable Arguments and Critique the Reasoning of Others

WHY CONSTRUCT AND CRITIQUE ARGUMENTS?

As mathematicians, we construct arguments based on our mathematical thinking. We justify our checking account totals using data we have recorded about our withdrawals and deposits. We argue that a restaurant bill is not accurate, relying on our understanding of the charges and our knowledge of math computations. We convince our children to wear their raincoats based on weather data, and we lay out our argument for when we must leave the house to get to an event on time. As we work to construct arguments, we use our math skills and knowledge to observe and interpret data, make conjectures about the data and the situation, and draw reasonable conclusions. As we listen to others' arguments, we consider, analyze, and continually use our math understanding to evaluate their arguments. Constructing and critiquing arguments are critical components of math proficiency.

UNDERSTANDING THE STANDARD

If our students give us the correct answer but are unable to explain how they got that answer or prove that the answer makes sense, would we be satisfied? Could they have memorized a process or formula without understanding what they are doing? Mathematically proficient students are able to do more than provide an answer. They are able to justify that answer and defend their process for finding the answer. They are able to share their reasoning, to prove that their actions and their answers make sense. Such students are able to assess others' thinking and recognize its validity or find faults in their arguments. And they are able to clearly communicate their thinking to others.

Mathematically proficient students are able to:

▸ construct viable arguments, both orally and in writing.

▸ listen to and critique the reasoning of others.

CONSTRUCTING ARGUMENTS

What do these tasks have in common?

Jan said that 6 is more than 4. Can you prove that?

Which unit of measure would you use to find the length of a pencil: inches, feet, or yards? Why?

Does 4 × 5 = 10 + 10? Why or why not?

Is 7 × 9 equal to (7 × 4) + (7 × 5)? Prove it.

Do we need zero in our number system? Why or why not?

Prove that 4.5 is equal to 4.50.

Jan multiplied 3.24 × 47.8 = 154872. Where should she put the decimal point in her product? Why?

Can a right triangle have an obtuse angle? Why or why not?

Each of the items above requires students to develop arguments to justify their thinking. Arguments are quite different from assertions. Our students often assert that their answer is correct "because it is," "because I know it," or "because I followed the steps." Their assertions simply state what they want us to believe without support or reasoning. Arguments, however, back up an answer or a statement with facts, data, or mathematical reasons to believe it. The act of constructing arguments challenges students to think about the math they are doing and often leads them to discover mistakes as well as insights while they struggle with the construction of their arguments.

Constructing viable arguments is not possible for students who lack an understanding of math skills and concepts. How many times has a student told you an answer, only to look totally confused when you begin to probe into how they got that answer or whether the answer makes sense? Understanding, or lack of understanding, is revealed when students are asked to defend their thinking. As students work to construct arguments, they consider math data and situations, and work to verbalize their reasoning.

Example A

Mrs. Hosty posted the following on the board:

$$4 \times 5 = 10 + 10$$

"Is that true?" she asked her third graders. "Before you answer, be sure you can tell me why."

Sara: $4 \times 5 = 20$ and $10 + 10 = 20$, so they are equal. They both are 20!

Teacher: Turn to your partner and tell if you agree or not.

Mrs. Hosty moved through the room, listening to her students. She heard Nicholas sharing a different perspective and asked him to share his idea.

Nicholas: I do think they are equal because a 10 is two 5s, so two 10s would be the same as four 5s. 4×5 is four 5s, and $10 + 10$ is like two 5s and another two 5s. They are saying the same thing!

Teacher: What do you think of Nicholas' thinking?

Sara: That would work, too, but I didn't think of that!

Students do not always defend their mathematical thinking in the same way. These students used different reasoning but were both able to defend their answers.

Example B

Mrs. Davis, a sixth-grade teacher, asked her students to find the product of 3.3 and 28.45. The class shared 9388.5, 93.885, 93.89, and 93,885 as possible solutions. These answers proved to be a catalyst for discussion and argument.

Teacher: We have quite a few possibilities. Which do you think is accurate?

Andrew: I think 9388.5. I just multiplied the numbers and moved the decimal place 3 spots. That's the shortcut for multiplying decimals.

Teacher: Who agrees with Andrew?

A few hands raised.

Teacher: Are there any other ideas?

Melissa: I just did the multiplication, but then I couldn't remember which way to move the decimal point. So I figured that 3.3 was about 3 and 28.45 was about 30.

Teacher: Why did you change the numbers?

Melissa: 3 and 30 are easy to multiply. I used easy numbers.

Mrs. Davis asked Melissa to record her thinking on the board before continuing. Melissa wrote the initial expression and her version with "easier" numbers.

Melissa: 3 times 30 is 90, so my answer had to be close to 90. When I looked at my product, 93885, I knew that the decimal point had to be between the 3 and 8. The product is 93.885 because that is close to 90.

Teacher: How many people couldn't remember which way to move the decimal point?

Close to half of the class raised their hands. Mrs. Davis then asked her students to talk with a partner about the strategy Melissa used to decide if it did or did not make sense and why. Melissa's ability to explain her procedure and reasoning got other students thinking about their own solutions and their own thinking.

While students most definitely need to understand math in order to defend their thinking, students also need language skills to construct strong arguments. Mathematically proficient students are effective communicators. They understand the math they do and are able to clearly communicate their ideas. They construct arguments by selecting important data, using specific examples, or citing logical reasoning to strengthen their points. Sara, Nicholas, and Melissa were able to verbalize their thinking, in an age-appropriate way, using specific examples, so others would understand.

CRITIQUING ARGUMENTS

When asked to critique the arguments of others, our students are being asked to actively listen to their classmates' thinking, evaluate their arguments, and make decisions as to whether they agree or disagree with their points. When we ask students to do this, we are challenging them to think at a high level and apply their math knowledge to assess someone else's argument. It is a productive classroom exercise as it strengthens our students' thinking skills and allows them to gain new perspectives and insights. It allows opportunities for students to consider ideas beyond their own as they analyze their classmates' arguments to either find fault in the arguments or become swayed by their classmates' logical conclusions.

Mr. Hill asked his second graders, "Do we need zero in our number system? Be ready to back up your answer with specific examples or reasons."

Mimi: We don't need zero because it is nothing.

John: Yeah—it doesn't matter if there is zero of something 'cause it just means there isn't any. You could just say none.

Amy: But what if you had 20 pieces of candy, but didn't have a zero? Then you would just have 2!

John: But the zero doesn't mean anything.

Amy: But it makes it a 20. Without the zero it is just 2 and that's not the same.

E.J.: And 50 and 500 need zeros or they are just 5. The zeros make different numbers.

Teacher: What do you mean different numbers?

Ellen: The zero moves the five to a different place in the number, so the number changes. 50 and 500 aren't the same.

Marty: That's what we do with the place value chart.

John: Okay, I think you need zero so you can make some numbers like 10 or 100.

Teacher: What do you think, Mimi?

Mimi: I think we need zero or we couldn't make a lot of numbers.

As Mimi and John listened to other students' reasoning and examples, they began to reconsider their initial ideas and changed their minds about the importance of zero.

Critiquing the ideas of others provides us with a window into our students' understanding. We see their ability to consider and judge the reasonableness of other answers and strategies.

Mr. Monroe posed the following problem to his seventh-grade students:

> *Perry has 2 cats, Claw and Callie. At the vet last year, Claw weighed 9 pounds and Callie weighed 14 pounds. At this year's vet visit, Claw weighed 12 pounds and Callie weighed 17 pounds. Did Claw or Callie grow more?*

After giving partners the opportunity to discuss the problem, Mr. Monroe asked the pairs to show their answer by moving to a side of the classroom (the left side for those who believed Claw grew more and the right side for those who believed Callie grew more). Partners began to confer and then some students moved to a side of the room while others stayed in their seats.

Teacher: So, who grew more? And why are some people still in the center of the room?

Sydney: They both grew the same. They both grew 3 pounds.

The students in the center nodded in agreement, adamant that they had done the subtraction and their results clearly supported that the cats' growth was the same.

Anna: But Claw only weighed 9 pounds before, so that was a lot for him to grow, but Callie weighed 14 pounds so gaining 3 pounds was not as much.

Marc: We didn't know which side of the room to go to, but Anna's answer makes sense so we should probably be over there.

Teacher: Explain what you mean.

Marc: They each grew 3 pounds but Callie weighed way more. So, even though they gained the same, Claw really grew more.

Mr. Monroe asked the partners to talk again and decide where they wanted to stand. He reminded them that it was okay to change their minds as long as they could justify why they were changing their answers. Other students chimed in with their agreement about Anna's perspective, although Sydney and her partner maintained that the cats' growth was the same. Through their arguments, Mr. Monroe assessed that some of his students were still additive thinkers (seeing only the actual pounds gained), while others were multiplicative thinkers (recognizing the difference in the cats' growth). He concluded that more discussion would be needed as they moved into their exploration of ratio.

REFINING STUDENTS' SKILLS

As with all of the Practice Standards, the ability to construct viable arguments and critique the reasoning of others is a process that begins at the primary level and continues to be refined throughout our students' school careers. Primary students begin to explain their thinking in simple ways. When we ask them questions like, "Why?" or "How do you know?" we encourage them to express their own thinking and listen to the thinking of others.

Figure 4.1 *This student begins his justification with a diagram to show his thinking.*

Young students use concrete materials or number lines to prove that 6 is more than 4 or that doubling 5 will make 10. They draw diagrams to prove that the answer to the problem must be 20 people because there are 2 round tables that each hold 6 people and 2 square tables that each hold 4 people (see Figure 4.1). We begin to challenge these students to use specific, grade-appropriate vocabulary, as well as their understanding of math concepts, to explain their thinking as they argue that 43 is more than 39 because there are 4 tens in 43 and only 3 tens in 39. They begin to include math definitions in their arguments as they argue that a rhombus must be a quadrilateral because it has 4 sides and that is what makes a quadrilateral.

We continue to probe with questions like, "Does that make sense?" and "Why is that true?" and encourage the development of students' evaluative skills with questions like, "Could that answer make sense?" or "Would Katie's way to solve the problem work? Why or why not?" With experience, our students begin to integrate their understanding of operations, properties, patterns, and formulas into their arguments and express their ideas using diagrams, expressions, equations, and inequalities, or citing data from charts, tables, and grade-appropriate graphs. They become skilled at listening to the arguments of others and are able to ask questions to clarify the arguments, identify faulty thinking, or suggest additions to strengthen the arguments. These Practices—of creating viable arguments and critiquing the reasoning of others—are developed in conjunction with math content skills throughout the K–8 years.

HOW DO WE GET THERE?
CLASSROOM-TESTED TECHNIQUES

What might we see in classrooms in which students are learning to construct and critique arguments? Following are some classroom-tested strategies that work for all levels of students.

Connections
to other practice standards

The structure of the activity is a problem in which students need to think critically and persevere (Standard 1).

Students reason quantitatively when considering numbers to eliminate from a problem set (Standard 2).

Students attend to the meaning of the concepts and terms and need to communicate precisely how they eliminated them (Standard 6).

Students apply patterns and generalizations to eliminate topics (Standard 8).

Eliminate It

In *Eliminate It* (O'Connell 2007a), students are presented with four math concepts and asked to decide on the one that should be eliminated, based on a mathematical fact or reason. Students are expected to state which item should be eliminated and add "because . . ." with clear reasoning or math data to back up their decision. If the argument is not clear, teacher probing guides the student to a more effective argument. There may be more than one way to eliminate an item, but each student is challenged to construct a clear argument for eliminating the item they select. The teacher continually asks the class if each response makes sense to them, ensuring that students listen to each other and assess the reasonableness of each response.

Example A

add	subtract
multiply	join

Blake: I would eliminate *join*, because *add*, *subtract*, and *multiply* are operations.

Teacher: Does that make sense?

Patrick: I would eliminate *subtract* because when you *add* or *multiply* you *join* things.

Teacher: Do you agree with Patrick?

Example B

rectangle	cylinder
circle	triangle

Jamie: I would eliminate *cylinder* because it is three-dimensional, and *rectangle*, *circle*, and *triangle* are two-dimensional figures.

Teacher: Would that work?

Kevin: I would eliminate *triangle*, because the net of a cylinder shows a rectangle and two circles.

Teacher: Do you agree with Kevin?

Eliminate It is a great strategy to get students thinking about numbers. Consider the following examples. Notice how teacher comments can guide students to elaborate on their responses and provide stronger arguments.

Example A

8	2
5	10

Colin: I would get rid of 5 because it is an odd number.

Teacher: How do you know it is odd?

Colin: Because if you used counters and put it in pairs you would have 1 left over, but you could put all the others in pairs and have none left over.

Liam: I would get rid of 10 because it is a two-digit number.

Teacher: How is that different from the other numbers?

Liam: They all have just one digit. Ten has a one in the tens place.

Bailey: I would get rid of 5 because the others are a fact family.

Teacher: Explain what you mean.

Bailey: $8 + 2 = 10$ or $10 - 2 = 8$ or $10 - 8 = 2$, but it doesn't work with a 5 in it. Just 2, 8, and 10.

Example B

21	63
17	84

Liz: I would eliminate 17 because it is a prime number.

Teacher: How do you know it is prime? How is that different from the others?

Liz: You can only get 17 with 1×17, but all of the others are composite and you can get them in other ways like $7 \times 3 = 21$ or $21 \times 3 = 63$ or $42 \times 2 = 84$.

Bobby: I would eliminate 84 because it is an even number.

Teacher: How could you prove that? Is that different from the others?

Bobby: It's the only one divisible by 2.

Carol: I would eliminate 17 because it isn't a multiple of 7.

Teacher: Are the others? Could you prove that?

Carol: $7 \times 3 = 21$ and $7 \times 9 = 63$ and $7 \times 12 = 84$.

Example C

$y + y + y$	$3y$
y^3	$2y + y$

Mary: I wanted to eliminate $y + y + y$ because it had addition.

Teacher: Is it the only one with addition?

Max: No, we thought about it, but it wouldn't work because $2y + y$ has addition, too.

Gilly: We decided to eliminate y^3 because it is the only one with an exponent.

Teacher: Would that work?

Brandy: Yes, you could do that, but we decided to get rid of y^3 because all of the others are the same.

Teacher: I am not sure I understand. Can you tell us more about your thinking?

Brandy: All of the expressions are the same. They give you the same answer. If you say $y = 5$, then $y + y + y = 15$ because $5 + 5 + 5 = 15$ and $3y = 15$ because $3 \times 5 = 15$ and $2y + y = 15$ because $(2 \times 5) + 5 = 15$, but $y^3 = 125$ because $5 \times 5 \times 5 = 125$. So we want to eliminate y^3.

Teacher: Would that work?

Students nodded after hearing Brandy's explanation.

Teacher: That was very specific, Brandy. Thanks for giving us examples and being so clear in your explanation.

Teacher questioning helps students identify the needed specificity of their responses. Teacher modeling, as well as discussions of various student responses, helps to refine students' skills in constructing effective justifications.

Eliminate It challenges students of all levels to find one of the four items that can be eliminated and then clearly communicate their reasoning to the rest of the class. It can be done as a whole-class activity, with students first sharing ideas with partners; in small, teacher-led groups to provide support to a small group of students as they learn to justify their answers; or as a written assignment for homework or classwork. And students' responses provide us with quick, formative assessment about their understandings, or misunderstandings, related to the math concepts.

Agree or Disagree?

In *Agree or Disagree*, the teacher poses a math statement, asking students to agree or disagree with the statement. Students must include math data or reasoning to support their decision. Following are examples of *Agree/Disagree* statements:

Jim has 12 pencils and Annie has 8. Jim has more than Annie.

7 + 3 and 4 + 6 are the only ways to make 10.

9 is an even number.

6 tens and 3 ones is the same as 5 tens and 13 ones.

6 dimes are worth more than 11 nickels.

$3\frac{1}{2}$ feet is more than 42 inches.

15 is a prime number.

3 jars of peanut butter for $7.50 is a better deal than 4 jars of peanut butter for $10.20.

A square is a rectangle.

Students might work with partners or in groups to decide whether they agree or disagree and then construct arguments to convince their classmates. Students were asked to agree or disagree with the statement that 75% is more than $\frac{2}{3}$. The student in Figure 4.2 agreed. To prove it, he converted 75% to $\frac{3}{4}$ so he could compare fractions and then included a diagram to show that $\frac{3}{4}$ is more than $\frac{2}{3}$. Another student converted $\frac{2}{3}$ to a percent to show 75% > 66%. Still another converted both to fractions with like denominators to prove that $\frac{9}{12}$ (75%) > $\frac{8}{12}$ ($\frac{2}{3}$).

Connections
to other practice standards

In order to agree or disagree, students need to calculate and communicate with precision (Standard 6).

Similar to *Eliminate It, Agree or Disagree* statements require students to employ problem-solving skills (Standard 1).

Students frequently model with mathematics to prove or disprove a statement (Standard 4).

Figure 4.2 *This student agrees that 75% is more than $\frac{2}{3}$, converting 75% to a fraction and then drawing a diagram to compare the fractions.*

Agree or Disagree?

75% is more than $\frac{2}{3}$.

Tell why you agree or disagree.

I agree that 75% is greater than $\frac{2}{3}$
75% is the same as $\frac{3}{4}$ because 4 25 make 100
and 75% is 3 25 $\frac{3}{4}$ is greater than $\frac{2}{3}$.

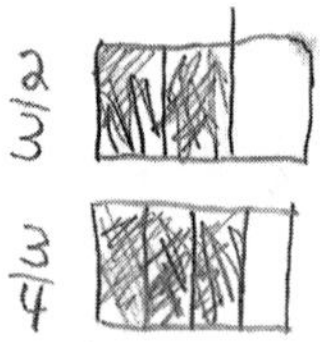

$\frac{2}{3}$ [diagram]

$\frac{3}{4}$ [diagram]

Figure 4.3 *This student disagrees that 5 nickels are worth more than 3 dimes. She provides information about the value of the coins and clearly explains her computations to prove her thinking.*

Agree or Disagree?

5 nickels are worth more than 3 dimes.

Tell why you agree or disagree.

I disagree because a dime is worth 10¢ and there are 3. 10+10+10=30. Nickels are worth 5¢ and there are 5 nickels. 5+5+5+5+5=25. 25¢ is less than 30¢.

Students share their arguments and consider the strengths of the arguments they have heard. Did they include examples, share logical reasoning, and/or cite pertinent math knowledge? After practicing with partners and in groups, challenge students to write arguments on their own, reminding them of what makes a good argument (see Figure 4.3). These make engaging warm-up tasks to begin the day, meaningful journal-writing tasks, and thoughtful homework assignments, as they challenge students to reflect deeply on the math content being taught.

My 2 Cents

Students benefit from reviewing the arguments of others and revising or expanding upon their ideas. In *My 2 Cents*, we provide sample arguments with flawed or incomplete logic. Students can work individually or with partners to improve the sample. It is critical that the class comes together to share ideas about revising arguments. In doing so, students see that there are different approaches to saying the same thing. This also helps us avoid the "teacher is always right" mentality when developing arguments in mathematics.

Consider simplifying $3x^2 - 3 - x^2 + 2x + 5 - 5x$. We could offer a sample argument that the simplified expression is $2x$ because $3x^2 - 3 = x^2$ and $x^2 - x^2 = 0$ and $0 + 2x$ is $2x$. Then we add $2x + 5$ and get $7x$, finally subtracting $7x - 5x$, which leaves us with $2x$. Obviously, our simplification disregards like terms. But in *My 2 Cents*, we allow students to critique the argument and develop a better, more mathematically appropriate, one (see Figure 4.4).

Connections
to other practice standards

Students consider the quantities and abstractions of the flawed statement (Standard 2).

Students may use models to attest why the statement is flawed (Standard 4).

Students may use patterns to disprove the statement (e.g., a statement that reads "not all products of two even factors are even" can be disproved by establishing the contrary pattern (Standard 7).

Figure 4.4   *This student critiques the argument and offers some ideas as to why it is faulty.*

My 2 Cents

$3x^2 - 3 + x^2 + 2x + 5 + 5x$ simplified is $2x$.

because...

$3x^2 - 3 = x^2$ ----> $x^2 - x^2 = 0$ ----> $2x + 5 = 7x$ ----> $7x - 5x = 2x$

This is way wrong. It just goes left to right. For example you can't do $3x^2 - 3$. They aren't like terms. You can only simplify with like terms. It should be $2x^2 + 2 - 3x$ or $2x^2 - 3x + 2$.

Give It a Try!

Students who have a clear understanding of the components of an effective argument are better able to construct arguments and critique the arguments of others. Arguments do not have to be lengthy, they simply need to be clear, specific, and contain data or reasoning to back up the thinking. That data might be in the form of computations, data charts or tables, diagrams, examples, and/or words that explain and prove the point being made.

Below is a list of sample questions at different grade levels. Select one that works for your students, or construct one of your own. Write a response that lacks thoroughness and specificity or that has faulty reasoning. Have students work with partners to critique the argument and decide how it can be improved. Record the following questions on the board to guide their work:

What should we keep? Why?

What should we delete? Why?

What should we add? How does that improve the argument?

Have pairs share their ideas. Is there more than one effective way to justify the response?

> **Which is worth more: 9 pennies or 3 nickels? Justify your answer.**
>
> **Which unit of measure would you use to find the length of a pencil: inches, feet, or yards? Why?**
>
> **Jenny has 2 bags of candy with 4 pieces in each bag. Ali has 3 bags of candy with 2 pieces in each bag. Who has more candy? Justify your answer.**
>
> **Which number belongs in the blank space on the hundred chart? Why? (include a hundred chart with one number covered)**
>
> **Why do we have to line up decimal points when adding?**
>
> **Why do we need a common denominator to add (or subtract) fractions?**
>
> **A 12" round pizza costs $6.50. A 10" x 14" rectangular pizza costs the same amount. Which pizza is the better buy? Support your answer with math data.**
>
> **Is 15 a prime or composite number? Justify your answer.**

ADDITIONAL IDEAS FOR DEVELOPING THE PRACTICE

How do we help our students to construct strong arguments that include specific math data and sound math reasoning? How do we help them listen to and assess the arguments of others?

Our students are better able to . . .	Because as teachers we . . .
Use assumptions, definitions, examples, counter-examples, and previously established results in constructing arguments.	Model effective arguments. Ask probing questions and supply wait time for students to elaborate on their arguments. Set high expectations for justifications (expect specificity, examples, and clear reasoning). Encourage students to construct arguments using concrete objects, diagrams, examples, definitions, and data. Use, and expect students to use, specific math vocabulary.
Justify conclusions, communicate them to others, and respond to the arguments of others.	Set up ongoing opportunities for students to defend their arguments, encouraging them to support their arguments with specific data and/or reasoning. Ask students to justify solutions, both orally and in writing, including the use of words, pictures, and numbers. Set up opportunities for students to communicate their arguments to others through oral presentations, partner discussions, or shared written work.
Reason inductively about data; make conjectures and build a logical progression of statements to explore the truth of their conjectures.	Ask students to observe data (e.g., equations, diagrams, charts, tables, graphs) and draw conclusions based on what is observed (i.e., display a row of parallelograms and ask students to describe a parallelogram based on observations). Model, and ask students to use, if/then reasoning (e.g., <u>if</u> a polygon has 4 sides, <u>then</u> it is a quadrilateral).

(continues)

Our students are better able to . . .	Because as teachers we . . .
Listen to or read the arguments of others, decide whether they make sense, and ask useful questions to clarify or improve the arguments.	Frequently ask specific questions as students share their answers in class, including, "Do you agree with . . .?" "Does that make sense?" "Even though Jen did it differently, does her way work?" Promote presentations and sharing sessions so students can share their arguments with others. Create student-to-student dialogue rather than relying solely on teacher-to-student discussions (e.g., "Do you agree with Katie's argument? Why or why not?"). Encourage students to ask questions to clarify classmates' arguments (e.g., "What did you mean by . . .?"). Create a nonthreatening classroom in which students feel safe to share their arguments and know how to ask clarifying questions and how to respectfully disagree with others.
Distinguish correct logic or reasoning from that which is flawed, and—if there is a flaw in an argument—explain what it is.	Give students opportunities to hear and critique each others' thinking. Ask students to pinpoint the data or mathematical reasoning that strengthens their arguments. Ask students to identify data or reasoning that may be flawed and identify how that data impacts the argument.

ASSESSMENT TIP

Oral discussions in which we model effective arguments, ask questions to prompt students' thinking, and highlight effective phrases, examples, or reasoning, allow students to gain insights about what it means to develop viable arguments. However, asking students to write justifications allows us to assess the level to which each student has mastered the skill. Using rubrics to score students' writing provides them with a guideline as they write and allows us to more accurately assess and more clearly share that assessment. A rubric score allows students to identify their strengths and determine ways to improve their writing. Figure 4.5 is a possible rubric for assessing

Figure 4.5   *Rubric for Student Justifications*

EXPECTED STUDENT OUTCOMES

The student is expected to create an argument to clearly justify an answer or clearly defend a mathematical decision. A clear justification includes the use of specific math vocabulary or symbolic notation and a logical organization so the argument can be understood. It also includes specific data, examples or counter-examples, diagrams, definitions, and/or explanations of the student's reasoning that support the answer or decision. Some complex arguments may require multiple pieces of evidence.

RUBRIC FOR A BRIEF JUSTIFICATION					
CATEGORY	**4**	**3**	**2**	**1**	**0**
Mathematical Reasoning	The argument does not contain flaws. There is specific and appropriate data or reasoning to support the student's decision/position. The argument contains at least one of the following: specific example and/or counter-example, a related definition, a labeled diagram, or other appropriate data to back up the main point. The student may include more than one way to justify his/her solution.	The argument may contain minor flaws. There is adequate data or reasoning to support the student's decision/position. The argument contains at least one of the following: an example, a definition, a diagram, or other appropriate data to back up the main point.	The argument may contain flaws. There is minimal data or reasoning to support the student's decision/position.	There is no mathematical reasoning or data to support the student's position/decision.	Blank; No response.
Communication	The writing is organized. The argument is presented in a clear, logical sequence. Precise math language and appropriate symbolic notation are evident.	The writing is generally clear and organized. It includes appropriate math language and symbolic notation.	The writing is somewhat organized but may lack clarity.	The writing may be difficult to understand and may not contain appropriate math language or symbolic notations.	Blank; No response.

student justifications. Keep in mind, there is not just one way to justify an answer or construct an argument. Students often successfully justify answers in ways we may not expect. We are looking for arguments that are clear, thorough, and convincing.

SUMMING IT UP

The National Council of Teachers of Mathematics' *Principles and Standards for School Mathematics* (2000) emphasizes the role that communication plays in learning mathematics. Talking and writing are critical processes through which students learn math content. When students construct mathematical arguments, they dig deep into their math understandings and, ultimately, build on those understandings. When they critique others' arguments, they apply their skills as mathematical thinkers to evaluate and assess others' thinking and, at the same time, extend their own. As students talk about, write about, and listen to math arguments, they are challenged to think, summarize, analyze, and refine their math understandings.

Exploring Standard 4:
Model with Mathematics

As we continue to explore the Standards for Mathematical Practice, it is important to remember that these standards describe student behaviors. As teachers, we model with mathematics routinely in our classrooms, but our goal is that our students are also able to model math ideas. Our job is to find ways to help our students develop this Practice. As we do so, we must be mindful that there are many ways to model a mathematical concept or strategy. In addition, while teacher modeling is a powerful instructional tool, our students will only develop this Practice if they are creating their own models or drawings.

WHY MODEL?

Models are representations of abstract math ideas. Through numbers, symbols, objects, diagrams, and graphic representations (e.g., charts, tables, graphs) we are able to see and manipulate math concepts and operations. Problem situations are clarified—and simplified—when we create models of the problem. We sketch out our floor plan when we go furniture shopping to be sure that our new furniture fits in the space. When posed with a brainteaser, we grab coins or toothpicks or anything we can get our hands on to model the complex puzzle, hoping to see it more clearly.

When we build an equation to represent what is happening in a problem, draw a diagram of a situation, pick up counters to model a problem, or create an organized table of problem data, we are finding ways to see the problem more clearly so we can work toward a solution. We visualize, simplify, and make sense of mathematics through models.

UNDERSTANDING THE STANDARD

When we ask our students to create math models, we challenge them to represent their math understanding—to get it out of their heads. They might do this by acting it out, using manipulatives, drawing diagrams, composing equations, or creating graphic representations (tables, charts, graphs, etc.). And as students look at their models, and the models that others have created, new insights arise, understanding is strengthened, and problems become simpler.

Mathematically proficient students are able to:

▶ model math ideas and problems in varied ways.

▶ analyze models to draw conclusions and solve problems.

CREATING MATH MODELS

When we think of creating math models, we tend to immediately think of geometry. Primary students create models of rectangles and squares using straws and marshmallows. Intermediate students explore angles as they model them with geoboards or AngLegs™, and middle grade students create and explore two-dimensional nets for three-dimensional figures in order to better understand the attributes of those figures or to explore the concepts of surface area and volume. But models are not just for geometry. In all areas of mathematics, creating models strengthens our students' understanding of math concepts and allows us to assess that understanding.

There are many ways to model math ideas and situations, whether those ideas relate to geometry, measurement, numbers, or algebra. Primary students might show an understanding of five by drawing 5 balloons, by putting 5 beans in a cup, or by placing 5 counters on a ten-frame. Intermediate students might model $\frac{2}{3}$ by partitioning a circular diagram into 3 parts and shading two of them or by folding a strip of paper into 3 equal lengths and labeling $\frac{2}{3}$ of the strip. Middle grade students might show the function $2n$ by displaying data on a function table (e.g., 2, 4; 3, 6; 4, 8; 5, 10 . . .) and creating a graph to represent the function.

Creating models of math problems is an invaluable skill for success in problem solving. When our students are able to get problems out of their heads through the creation of models, solutions are often not far behind.

The following problem was posed to first-grade students:

11 horses are in a field.

6 are black.

The rest are brown.

How many horses are brown?

Emma drew a picture to model the problem (see Figure 5.1). She accurately represented the problem, drawing 11 circles to represent horses and then coloring 6 of them black. She then counted the remaining circles to find that 5 horses were brown.

Figure 5.1 *This primary student models a problem with a simple drawing that accurately represents the problem situation.*

Emma's classmate Jack simply wrote the equation 11 − 6 = 5. When questioned by his teacher, Jack was able to explain what 11 and 6 represented and why he chose to subtract. "Because I needed to know how many the other part was. There were 6 black horses and I needed to know the brown part. You just subtract. It's 11 together."

Madison created a model of the problem with cubes, selecting 11 cubes and then putting 6 of them together. "They're the black ones," she explained. She counted the remaining cubes and confidently stated that 5 horses were brown because she "showed it." The equation, the drawing, and the manipulatives effectively modeled the problem situation. In all cases, the data was accurate and the understanding of the operation (the action of the problem) was evident.

ANALYZING MODELS

While the ability to create appropriate models is important, it is equally important that our students can analyze their models to gain insights, draw conclusions, and solve problems. When primary students model five by placing 5 counters on a ten-frame, they discover that 5 is half of 10 and that 5 is more than 4, but less than 6. The intermediate student who models $\frac{2}{3}$ discovers that it is more than $\frac{1}{2}$, but less than $\frac{3}{4}$.

The middle grade student who sees the line form as he plots the values for $2n$ on his graph, recognizes a linear function.

Mrs. O'Connor posed the following problem to her first graders:

> *Kelly was in line to buy lemonade. There were 3 people in front of her in the line. There were 2 people behind her in the line. How many people were waiting in line to buy lemonade?*

Many of her students saw the 3 and 2 in the problem and combined the data, deciding that 5 people were in line to buy lemonade, but Rosie opted to model the problem. She grabbed a counter to represent Kelly and placed 2 counters in front of it and 3 counters behind it. Counting her row of counters, Rosie declared that 6 people were in line. Many of her classmates disagreed because "2 + 3 = 5," so Mrs. O'Connor suggested that the class act out the problem. As the students looked at the human model they had formed in front of the class, their insights were immediate. "We forgot Kelly!" one student exclaimed! Benny wisely added that "the number sentence should be 2 + 3 + 1 because we have to add Kelly."

The following problem was posed to a fourth-grade class:

> *Jack and Jill shared a pizza. Jack ate $\frac{1}{3}$ of the pizza and Jill ate $\frac{1}{2}$ of the pizza. How much of the pizza was left?*

Eventually, students will work with common denominator algorithms, but understanding through modeling is the definitive starting place. Drawings, paper folding or cutting, and manipulatives are all reasonable ways to model the problem. One approach may be to use pattern blocks, with the yellow hexagon representing a whole pizza (see Figure 5.2). A blue rhombus represents the amount of pizza Jack ate ($\frac{1}{3}$), while a red trapezoid represents the amount Jill ate ($\frac{1}{2}$). As our students build a model of this problem by placing the rhombus and trapezoid together, they are better able to determine the missing part of the

Figure 5.2 *These students gain insights about the problem by analyzing their fraction model.*

pizza. Our careful questions can then help them analyze the model to figure out the mathematics. We might ask:

Are there any pattern blocks that fit that space (triangle)?

How many triangles are needed to make the trapezoid and the rhombus?

Could we show the amount Jack and Jill ate using triangles? What would that be?

What would be an equation that goes with our model?

Through this task, students build a fraction model and then use it to discover the solution to the problem.

Mr. Newell's seventh graders were posed the following problem:

> **A plane is traveling at 400 miles per hour. How far will it travel in 6 hours?**

Brian was initially confused about the problem, and so he drew the diagram in Figure 5.3. Brian's diagram helped him visualize the problem and more clearly view the data. He correctly found that the plane traveled 2,400 miles in 6 hours and, after reflecting on his model, the algorithm to solve the problem became clear. Creating the model allowed Brian to visualize the problem and gain insights toward the solution.

Figure 5.3 *This student created a model to organize his thoughts about the problem.*

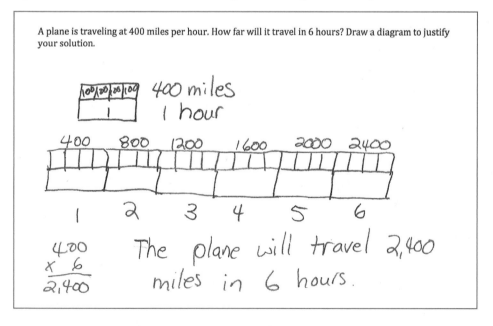

HOW DO WE GET THERE?

CLASSROOM-TESTED TECHNIQUES

Model It

Give students lots of experience constructing math models. Provide some manipulatives and paper and pencils. Then challenge students to find a way to show their understanding of a quantity or an expression by using the manipulatives or creating drawings. At all grade levels, students are challenged to think about the math and determine a way to represent it. Have students create their own models and then share with a partner to see how each of their models is alike or different. Would both models work with the math concept? Share some of their models with the whole class to allow students to see multiple ways the math could be represented, as in the following examples.

Model 4

▸ Jacob drew 4 circles.

▸ Ali put 4 beans on a mat.

Model 123 + 57

▸ Sam used base-ten blocks to show 123 as 1 flat (hundred), 2 rods (tens) and 3 units (ones). He showed 57 as 5 rods and 7 units. He explained that since he was adding, he needed to put three of the units from the 123 with the 7 units from the 57. Then he traded those 10 units for another rod. He counted the 2 rods (tens) from 123 and the 5 rods from 57 (and added the one he made from the units) to get 8 rods (tens). He counted the 1 hundred, 8 tens, and 0 ones to get 180.

▸ Annie drew a picture to show 123 + 57 (see Figure 5.4).

Figure 5.4   *This student shows her understanding of 123 + 57 through her drawing. She adds an additional rod (ten) after seeing that there are a total of 10 ones.*

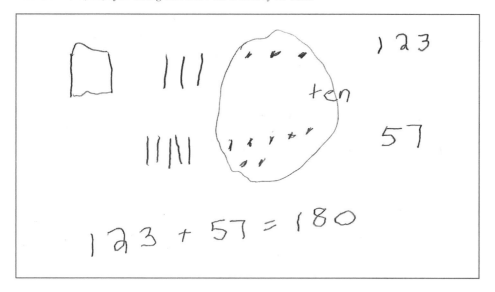

Model 3.5

▶ Stephanie used base-ten blocks to show 3.5. When using base-ten blocks for decimals, the flat (100 block) can represent 1 whole, the rod (10 block) can represent 1 tenth, and the unit (1 block) can represent 1 hundredth. Stephanie showed 3.5 with 3 flats (wholes) and 5 rods (tenths). She struggled a bit when modeling the decimal with base-ten blocks as she had to readjust her thinking from her past experiences representing whole numbers with the same blocks.

▶ Maria shaded 10 × 10 grids to model 3.5. She completely shaded three grids, as well as 5 columns of ten on the fourth grid. She noted that the 3 represented the number of wholes and explained that there were "100 *smalls* in one whole square," explaining that the *smalls* were arranged in columns of 10. She explained that, "the .5 means 5 tenths, that's 5 columns, so I need those and the 3 wholes."

▶ Luci showed 3.5 on a number line (see Figure 5.5). She marked the point halfway between 3 and 4 as 3.5 and shared her thinking.

Figure 5.5 *This student modeled 3.5 on a number line and explained her thinking.*

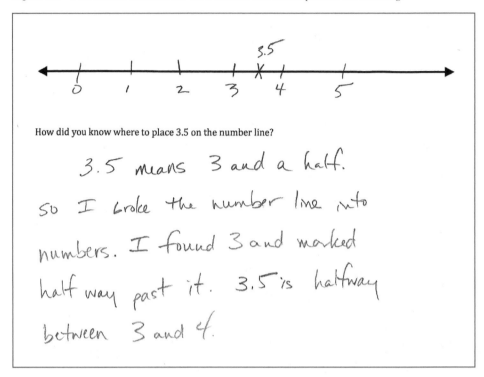

How did you know where to place 3.5 on the number line?

3.5 means 3 and a half. So I broke the number line into numbers. I found 3 and marked half way past it. 3.5 is halfway between 3 and 4.

Model $1 - \frac{1}{3}$

- ▶ Kym partitioned a number line with the endpoints of 0 and 1 into thirds. She noted 1 as her starting point and jumped back $\frac{1}{3}$ and marked the spot. She then identified that point as $\frac{2}{3}$, showing that $1 - \frac{1}{3} = \frac{2}{3}$.

- ▶ Aidan partitioned a number line with endpoints of 0 and 1 into thirds. He started at $\frac{1}{3}$ and counted the thirds up to 1. He explained that there are 2 thirds between $\frac{1}{3}$ and 1, so the difference between 1 and $\frac{1}{3}$ was $\frac{2}{3}$.

- ▶ Krissy drew a rectangle and partitioned it into thirds, explaining that she chose to split it into thirds because that was the amount that she was taking away. As Krissy lightly shaded $\frac{1}{3}$, she shared that it was the amount taken away. After shading the region, Krissy stated, "We had 1 whole and took away $\frac{1}{3}$, so we're left with $\frac{2}{3}$. $1 - \frac{1}{3} = \frac{2}{3}$."

Model 3.4 + 5.07

▸ Jackson added 3.4 and 5.07 as if they represented money. He showed 3.4 as 3 dollars and 40 cents, adding a zero to the hundredths column. He showed 5.07 as 5 dollars and 7 cents. He then exclaimed that it was easy to add the dollars and cents separately, 3 + 5 is 8 dollars and 40 + 7 is 47 cents.

▸ Tyson added these numbers with 10 × 10 grids. He shaded 3 whole grids and 4 columns of another. He then shaded 5 whole grids and 7 small squares of another. Tyson then added the wholes and parts separately, first adding the 3 and 5 wholes to get 8 wholes. He then added the parts, 40 hundredths and 7 hundredths, and totaled the two amounts to find the sum: 8.47.

Model 2n + 1

▸ Annie examined the expression and drew 3 rectangles. She wrote an *n* in the first 2 rectangles and a 1 in the last rectangle. Annie explained that she could replace the *n* with any value and just add all of the values together. She demonstrated this with an 8. She said, "If *n* equals 8, I would have 2 eights, which is 16 and then I would add 1. So if *n* equaled 8, 2*n* + 1 would equal 17."

Give It a Try!

Ask your students to model some quantities or expressions that are grade-level appropriate. Remember that students approach models in different ways. You are looking for models that accurately represent the math concepts, even if they might not be what you had in mind. Be sure to provide opportunities for students to share their models with classmates. Consider prompts such as the following:

▸ Model 3 + 1

▸ Model 27 − 15

▸ Model 123 + 57

▸ Model $3\frac{1}{4}$

▸ Model 4.5

▸ Model 40% of 30

▸ Model 3*n* = 36

Problem-Solving Models

Introduce your students to some problem-solving models to help them identify the important information and visualize the action of the operations. Part-part-whole mats can be a helpful way for students to visualize addition and subtraction. For multiplication and division problems, bar diagrams offer helpful visuals.

Part	Part
Whole	

PART-PART-WHOLE MATS FOR ADDITION AND SUBTRACTION   Mrs. King's kindergarten class explored the following problems using their part-part-whole mats and counters. After each problem was posed, the students worked with partners to place the counters for the known information on their mats and then used their understanding of parts and whole to find the unknown information.

There were 2 yellow lollipops and 3 red lollipops. How many lollipops were there?

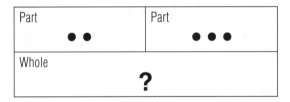

Students placed the parts in each section and moved the parts together to find the whole.

There were 6 children. 3 were boys. How many were girls?

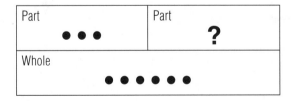

Students placed the known parts (3) and the whole (6) on their mats and then compared to find the difference (the unknown part). Students were able to move the counters, lining them up to see the one-to-one correspondence, when solving and checking their answers.

> *There were 5 cupcakes. Jan ate some. There were 2 left. How many did she eat?*

Part ?	Part • •
Whole • • • • •	

Students again practiced finding the missing part by comparing the known part to the whole.

Part-part-whole mats provide a simple model for joining parts to create the whole or for comparing the whole to the known part in order to find the missing part.

BAR DIAGRAMS FOR MULTIPLICATION AND DIVISION   Bar diagrams are models that are useful for computation and problem solving. The construction of simple bar diagrams allows intermediate students to visualize multiplication and division. Students create a bar for the total amount and bars to represent the parts or groups. Let's take a look at these models with three distinct word problems.

> *Problem 1: There are 3 boxes with 6 toys in each box. How many toys are there?*

In this unknown product problem, we know the number of parts (3) and the amount in each part (6). So we have 3 bars of 6. The total is unknown (?), yet equivalent to 3 bars of 6. The bar diagram looks something like this:

6	6	6

?

Connections
to other practice standards

Bar diagrams help students visualize problems and make sense of them (Standard 1).

Bar diagrams help students compose arguments to justify their process or solution (Standard 3).

Using a bar diagram supports students' precise calculation when solving problems (Standard 6).

Students may notice the repetition of action words and gain insight into the operations they indicate (Standard 8).

Problem 2: 18 toys are packed equally in 3 boxes. How many toys are in each box?

In this problem, the size of each group is unknown. The diagram shows the total amount of toys (18) and their equivalence to 3 boxes, or groups. The amount in each box is unknown.

?	?	?

18

Problem 3: 18 toys are packed 6 to a box. How many boxes are needed?

In Problem 3, we know the total (18) and the size of each group (6). We do not know how many groups will be created. Creating a bar diagram with a total of 18 and boxes of 6 helps to show the number of boxes needed. This problem can be solved by thinking about $? \times 6 = 18$, $18 \div 6 = ?$, or how many 6s will total 18?

6	6	6

18

BAR DIAGRAMS FOR SOLVING EQUATIONS   Many of our middle school students struggle with solving equations. For some, the procedures are muddled because the mathematical meaning of an equation is misunderstood. Diagrams help these students make sense of an equation and solve for the unknown. Consider the equations $18 = 2x$ and $4x - 3 = 25$. A diagram of each can help promote meaning and improve accuracy.

We can show $18 = 2x$ with the bar diagram below:

18	
x	*x*

A conversation about this model may center on the questions:

How many xs are there?

What is the total value of the xs? How do you know?

How could we figure out the value of 1 x?

What would a picture or diagram of this equation look like?

We can show $4x - 3 = 25$ with the bar diagram below:

X	X	X	X
25			3

Questions for our students to consider might include:

Is 4x more than or less than 25?

How much less is it? How do you know?

So 25 and some more make 4x? How much more?

How could we show that with a picture or diagram?

Technology Tools

While in the past, we have relied on chart paper and markers to show math ideas, now we have increasingly more options with the technology tools and electronic manipulatives that are available today. Look for websites, like the National Council of Teachers of Mathematics' *Illuminations* site (http://illuminations.nctm.org/), in which electronic manipulatives are available for students to explore and maneuver. Sites like this allow students to create models using applets that are specifically directed to our learning goals.

STUDENT BEHAVIORS AND TEACHER ACTIONS

Do students have opportunities to model their mathematical thinking? Do you discuss how models have helped them find solutions or gain insights? Expand on what you are already doing with some of the suggestions shown on the next page.

ADDITIONAL IDEAS FOR DEVELOPING THE PRACTICE

Our students are better able to . . .	Because as teachers we . . .
Make models to simplify a situation.	Model the use of diagrams and drawings to represent problems. Encourage students to create simple diagrams to show problems. Facilitate discussions in which students share multiple ways to model mathematics. Encourage students to revise diagrams as needed.
Identify models that are most efficient for solving specific problems or representing specific math ideas.	Discuss specific models and their value. (e.g., Why use base-ten blocks to show 27? Why does a 10×10 grid work well to represent a decimal?) Discuss times when a specific model might be appropriate (e.g., Would a 10×10 grid also be appropriate to model percents? Fractions? Why?) Ask students to explain why they chose a particular model.
Analyze models and draw conclusions based on what they see.	Consistently ask for their insights after looking at models. Ask students to interpret models for their classmates (i.e., describe or explain their model). Have students write about what they learned from their model.

ASSESSMENT TIP

Student interviews, both formal and informal, provide us with specific data about our students' understanding of math concepts, as well as their ability to create models of those concepts. As students are working on constructing models during a classroom activity, we might simply stop to observe and ask questions to check their understanding. This spontaneous, informal interview can yield insights about their reasoning and skills. Formal interviews might be done at a specific time during which students bring their model to our desk and we pose questions like the following:

Tell me what your model represents.

Why did you choose this model?

Did creating a model help you in any way? If so, how?

Did you get any insights by looking at your model?

Is there another way you might model this problem or idea? How?

Interviews are an effective way to assess our students' thinking as they show, explain, and justify their models.

SUMMING IT UP

Creating models challenges our students to delve into their understanding of math ideas in order to represent them. Primary students represent real-life situations using actions, objects, drawings, number lines, words, and numbers. As our students develop their skills, they continue to rely on those models to make sense of math, but add charts, tables, and graphs to their repertoire, relying on them to help organize data so they can better understand it, analyze it, and draw conclusions about it. From grades K–8, our students use models to clarify math concepts and simplify math problems.

6

Exploring Standard 5:
Use Appropriate Tools Strategically

A re you thinking that there seems to be a great deal of overlap in these standards? In Standard 2, we talked about the connections between abstract thinking (equations) and real situations (problems). Or was that Standard 1, where we talked about building equations as one of the strategies students use to solve problems? But wait. In Standard 4, we explored modeling math ideas and again mentioned equations, concrete materials, and diagrams as ways to model math concepts. If we attempt to place each of these standards in a separate compartment, we will surely become frustrated and confused.

These standards explore and explain the practices of good mathematicians, and when we perform any task, particularly one as complex as math, our actions cannot be simplified into compartments. Each standard has a unique focus, but each standard also intermingles with the others as we put it into practice. Rather than trying to compartmentalize these Practices, think about blending the Practices to empower your students to use math and to think mathematically.

WHY FOCUS ON TOOLS?

Mathematicians use tools to do their work. When performing calculations we must decide if we should use paper and pencil, grab a calculator, or do mental math to find the solution. When measuring, we must determine which tool to use and which unit of measure makes the most sense for the task. Should we measure the length and width of our walls with a ruler and bring measurements in inches to the store to determine the amount of wallpaper we need, or might measurements in feet or yards be more helpful? Should we grab a blank sheet of paper or choose grid paper to create a model of our floor plan prior to buying new furniture to fit in a room? Mathematicians are familiar with a variety of tools, are able to determine which tool makes sense for a given task, and can effectively use the tool to perform that task.

UNDERSTANDING THE STANDARD

Mathematics is an active discipline. The ability to select and use mathematical tools is essential for our students' success in performing many tasks. Whether they are adding quantities, measuring a perimeter, calculating the weight of an object, or determining the measure of angles, our students meet with greater success if they can identify appropriate tools to support each task and effectively use those tools to perform the task.

While we may immediately think of tools as math devices like rulers, compasses, protractors, and calculators, the CCSS Standards for Mathematical Practice have a much broader definition of *tools*. Tools are what support students to perform a task. Concrete materials like base-ten blocks, connecting cubes, and 10×10 grids can be tools, so can grid paper, number lines, and hundred charts. Calculators, pencil and paper, and even mental math are also tools. Some of these items were explored in the previous chapter as models, but they can also be classified as tools when they help us perform tasks, find solutions, or solve problems. Tools enhance our students' mathematical power by assisting them as they perform tasks.

Mathematically proficient students:

▸ decide when to use tools and select appropriate tools.

▸ use tools appropriately and accurately.

SELECT APPROPRIATE TOOLS

Mathematicians choose tools that help them make sense of math and solve math problems. Primary students might select tools like counters, number lines, and hundred charts to help them solve math problems. What might they use to add $5 + 2$? Cubes? A number line? A ten-frame and counters? What might they use to measure and compare the length of two objects? Connecting cubes? A ruler?

There is often more than one tool that will work for a task, but some tools are more efficient than others and students begin to decide which tools will best meet their needs. With each grade level, more tools are introduced. Should students measure with a yardstick or a ruler? Which will give them the most useful information? While we teach algorithms, when are the paper/pencil algorithms the best way to solve a problem and when might a calculator or mental math be quicker and easier? The ability to select appropriate tools is an important reasoning skill.

Mrs. Morley put the following on the board:

1.NBT.4

17 + 4

She used a think-pair-share approach to get all of her students thinking and talking about the expression. She asked her first-grade students to think about the answer and think about how they got the answer. After a few seconds, she asked them to turn to their partners, whisper the answer, and explain how they got it. She listened as they shared their approaches with partners. Finally, she asked the students to share as a class.

Megan: I wrote the numbers down on my paper. I put 17 on top of 4 and then I added the ones and got 11, so I wrote the 1 and then put the other 1 in the tens place, then I added the tens. I got 21.

Teacher: Do you agree with Megan's answer?

Students nodded.

Teacher: Did anyone do it another way?

Colleen: I got 21, too, but I just started with 17 and counted on 4.

Teacher: You didn't write it on paper?

Colleen: No.

Teacher: Why not?

Colleen: I could just add on. I didn't need to.

Teacher: Did anyone else do it without paper?

Lisa: I didn't use paper. I just knew 7 + 4 was 11, so I thought it's just 10 + 11 and that's 21!

Teacher: Does that make sense?

Mike: It does, but I didn't do it like that. I just thought that you need 3 more to make 20 and then you would have 1 left, so it's 21.

Teacher: So, you could have used a paper and pencil, but you also could have done this in your head in lots of different ways?

Betsy: Yeah. And it was faster in my head!

Many of Mrs. Morley's students recognized the value of mental math as a tool for solving that problem.

In Ms. Hall's fourth-grade class the problem was:

$$2\tfrac{1}{2} + 1\tfrac{1}{2} = \underline{\quad\quad}$$

4.NF.3

In much the same way, several of Ms. Hall's students described the lengthy written computation as they converted each fraction to a mixed number ($2\tfrac{1}{2} = \tfrac{5}{2}$ and $1\tfrac{1}{2} = \tfrac{3}{2}$) and then added $\tfrac{5}{2} + \tfrac{3}{2}$ to get a sum of $\tfrac{8}{2}$, then divided to find the answer: 4. But Julie simply used mental math to add the whole numbers and then added the fractions, explaining that "2 + 1 is 3 and $\tfrac{1}{2}$ and $\tfrac{1}{2}$ is one more, so it is 4." Julie selected mental math as the tool to efficiently find the answer.

In intermediate and middle school mathematics classrooms, we may see:

▸ Jennifer select grid paper to sketch the unusual shape of the playground, so she can better calculate its perimeter.

▸ Chris use a function table to convert feet to meters to complete his task.

▸ Amy use a graphing calculator to show the relationship between the number of books purchased and the total cost.

▸ Carol select a protractor to measure the angles of various polygons as she explores the sum of the angles in polygons.

▸ Ali select a calculator to compare compound and simple interest problems.

Our students are constantly faced with decisions about which tools will effectively help them complete math tasks. Can they select the appropriate measurement tool (linking cubes, ruler, yardstick, protractor, balance scale) to perform a task? Can they select construction tools (compass, grid paper, straight edge, tiles, or blocks) that make sense for various tasks? Can they select computational tools (paper/pencil, number line, calculator, mental math) to help them most efficiently perform the computations? Our students benefit from opportunities to select a tool that makes sense for the math task and to evaluate which tool is most efficient for that task.

USE TOOLS APPROPRIATELY

Not only do our students need to be able to select appropriate tools, they must be able to effectively use those tools. A student who grabs a calculator to perform the operation 3.156 × 76.324 has chosen a tremendously helpful tool, since the computation is lengthy. However, the student runs the risk of error if he does not accurately enter the numbers and decimal points into the calculator. The chances of a resulting error are high for students who lack skill with a tool, or for those who do not use their number sense to check the reasonableness of the answer generated by the tool. Do our students simply record the answer seen on the calculator display, or do they check their answer for reasonableness?

> **Pat:** Let's see, 3 × 75 is about 225, so the answer should be close to that. 240.866 is close. That sounds right!

> **Joe:** 24.087 isn't even close. Wait, what just happened?

Tools must be used effectively to be helpful to students.

Do students know how to use number lines?

- ▶ Where do they begin on the number line?
- ▶ What direction should they move?
- ▶ How do they know the quantity for each "jump"?

Do students know how to use rulers?

- ▶ Where do they place the ruler on the object to be measured?
- ▶ Do the markings begin at the edge of the ruler, or is there an indentation before the measurement markings begin?
- ▶ Do they understand that the length is the difference between 2 points on the ruler, not just the distance from 0 to another point on the ruler?
- ▶ Do they understand the fractional markings in order to be able to read the measurement?

Do students know how to use protractors?

▶ Do they know how to accurately place the protractor on one of the rays?

▶ Do they understand the concepts of acute and obtuse, thus determining which of the two measurements is the appropriate one for the angle they are measuring?

▶ Do they understand that the protractor measures the rotation of one segment or ray from another ray?

Do students know how to use graphing calculators?

▶ Do they understand how to input the data?

▶ Can they manipulate the data that is graphed?

▶ Are they able to follow button procedures to complete tasks?

▶ Can they make sense of the representations and apply them to different situations?

▶ Do they understand concepts of linear equations, slope, and functions and the resulting graphs?

Explicit instruction in the use of tools, discussion of the common errors related to specific tools, and ongoing practice with tools all contribute to our students' mastery of math tools.

HOW DO WE GET THERE?

CLASSROOM-TESTED TECHNIQUES

Number Lines as Tools

Number lines are powerful tools for computation and estimation tasks. In primary classrooms, number lines help students determine the next number in a counting sequence and help them add or subtract whole numbers. In intermediate classrooms, number lines help students compare the values of fractions or decimals. Number lines support middle grade students through their struggles with understanding and performing computations with positive and negative values.

Number lines help students see numbers in a sequence, allowing them to determine approximate values (e.g., it's about $3\frac{1}{2}$) or make comparison statements (e.g.,

Connections
to other practice standards

Number lines support students' precise calculations (Standard 6).

Number lines provide students with data and support when constructing arguments (Standard 3).

Number lines highlight number patterns (Standard 7).

Connections
to other practice standards

It's Close To . . .
invites rich classroom
discussion and reasoning
(Standard 3).

It's Close To . . .
improves students'
ability to reason
quantitatively by
improving their
number sense
(Standard 2).

4.NF.2

that one value is greater than or less than another). Having appropriate number lines available as problem-solving tools supports a variety of students who struggle with conceptual understanding and who will benefit from visualizing the process they are performing.

IT'S CLOSE TO . . .   With the help of a fraction number line, students can easily compare $\frac{3}{5}$ and $\frac{2}{8}$ without finding a common denominator or cross-multiplying. By simply thinking of each number's placement on a number line, the comparison becomes clear: $\frac{3}{5}$ is more than half, since 2.5 would be half of 5. $\frac{2}{8}$ is less than half, since $\frac{4}{8}$ would be half. It is clear then that $\frac{3}{5} > \frac{2}{8}$. The ability to view the quantities on a number line proves the comparison.

It's Close To . . . is an activity that gives students practice using a number line as they determine if fractions are closer to 0, $\frac{1}{2}$, or 1, and then justify their decision. Using a 0–1 fraction number line allows students to visually explore each fraction as they find its location on the number line. In Figure 6.1, a student says $\frac{1}{6}$ is closer to 0. She establishes that half is $\frac{3}{6}$ and puts $\frac{1}{6}$ just a little past 0 on her number line. Friendlier denominators, like 4, 5, 6, 8, and 10, allow students to practice with fractions that are simpler to place on the number line. After some practice, students are ready to explore more complex fractions such as $\frac{3}{19}$, $\frac{8}{11}$, or $\frac{20}{21}$.

Figure 6.1   *This number line clearly shows that $\frac{1}{6}$ is closer to 0.*

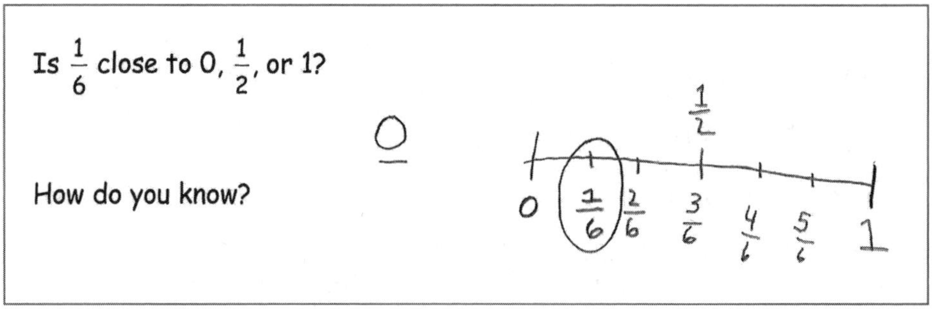

Students
might also be asked
to place decimals
on a 0–1 number
line to determine if
they are closer to
0, $\frac{1}{2}$, or 1 (e.g., Is
.85 closer to 0, $\frac{1}{2}$,
or 1? Justify
your answer).

Rulers as Tools

The ability to use a tool correctly is dependent on our students' understanding of the purpose of the tool, as well as their understanding of the math concepts related to that tool. Even basic tools, such as rulers, present problems for our students either because they don't have a clear understanding of the tool's purpose (to measure length), or they are confused about related math concepts (like the fractional markings on the ruler).

Rulers are frequently used math tools. A common error occurs when our students do not accurately align the beginning of the ruler (0 on the number line) with the beginning of the object they are measuring. Their measurements are slightly inaccurate because they are measuring from the end of the ruler, rather than from the actual markings on the ruler. Attention to this common error, and practice in finding the starting point on different styles of rulers, minimizes this error. However, this error highlights a greater concern. Do our students realize that they do not even need to start at 0 on a ruler to get an accurate measurement? Length is the distance between two points, or the difference between the starting and ending points. A pencil is 6 inches long, regardless of where we start our measurement on the ruler. If we measure from 0 to 6, 2 to 8, or 5 to 11, the measurement is still 6 inches.

Even those students who understand the concept of measuring length can struggle using rulers. A ruler is a number line, with points between whole numbers, so measuring objects that are not whole units can be a challenge. Errors occur when our students attempt to name the measurement as they look at the hash marks on the ruler. Is it $2\frac{1}{4}$ inches? Or $2\frac{3}{8}$ inches? What do those hash marks mean? Our students' confusion about fractions, and their relation to the hash marks, leads to inaccurate measures.

THE BROKEN RULER   Have you ever tried to measure something with a broken ruler? Have you ever tried to use a ruler to measure something longer than 12 inches? How did you measure the object in those instances? Broken ruler tasks help students develop an understanding of how to use a ruler flexibly and appropriately. In these tasks, students measure objects using hypothetical *broken rulers*. These rulers can be "broken" at either end—they either don't begin with 0 or don't end with 12 (see Figure 6.2 and Appendix C). Students must find a way to accurately measure an object, despite the broken tool. This requires understanding of the tool, reasoning skills, and calculation skills. Have students work with partners to develop a plan to measure the objects, do the measuring, and then construct arguments to support their measurements (see Figure 6.3).

EXPLORING A MAGNIFIED INCH   Student's accuracy with using rulers is linked to their understanding of fractions. Have you explored rulers as a fraction number line? Students can create a magnified inch (see Figure 6.4) by folding a sentence strip in half,

Connections
to other practice standards

Students are confronted with a rich problem when trying to measure an object with a broken ruler (Standard 1).

Students gain the insight that measurement is the difference between two points. They can apply this to other concepts, including subtraction (Standard 8).

Figure 6.2   *Could your students measure objects using these broken rulers?*

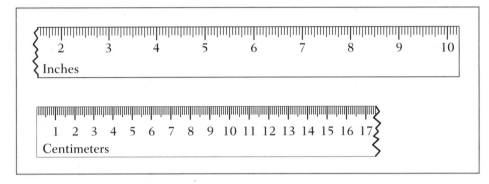

Figure 6.3   *These students must use their reasoning skills, as well as their understanding of rulers, to measure the width of the crayon box using a broken ruler.*

Figure 6.4   *Students explore fractions as they create a magnified inch.*

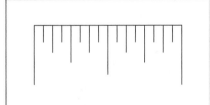

opening it, and marking $\frac{1}{2}$ at the center fold. Then have them refold the strip in half and fold it in half again. Have students open the sentence strip and label $\frac{1}{4}$, $\frac{2}{4}$, $\frac{3}{4}$ on the three folds of the paper. Can students describe what they see?

Are the sections equal in size?

Do the fraction labels make sense? Why?

Where is 0? Why?

Where is 1? Why?

Why are $\frac{1}{2}$ and $\frac{2}{4}$ on the same fold?

Have students refold the paper and then fold it in half one more time. When they open the paper, have them place a mark on each fold and indicate what each of the new marks represents ($\frac{1}{8}, \frac{2}{8}, \frac{3}{8}, \frac{4}{8}, \frac{5}{8}, \frac{6}{8}, \frac{7}{8}$). Stop and discuss the measurements.

Why is there more than one fraction on some folds?

Does it make sense that those fractions are on the same fold? Why?

Which of those fractions is easiest to understand? Would you say $\frac{1}{2}$ or $\frac{2}{4}$ or $\frac{4}{8}$? Why?

If appropriate, make another fold and mark sixteenths. Have them practice identifying the correct measurements as one partner places a counter on a spot on the magnified inch and the other states the appropriate measurement in fractions of an inch.

Once students have become comfortable with the magnified inch, have them compare their magnified inch to the markings on a ruler. How are they alike? How are they different? Recognizing that each set of markings between the whole numbers on a ruler look the same and represent the same fractions of a whole helps students identify $2\frac{1}{2}$ or $4\frac{3}{4}$.

The understanding of equivalent fractions enhances our students' abilities to use rulers accurately as they are able to understand that $\frac{14}{16}$ of an inch is the same as $\frac{7}{8}$ of an inch. While an understanding of fractions helps students accurately use rulers, the use of rulers also helps students better understand fractions, since rulers are a linear model, sometimes called a measurement model, of fractions.

DEVELOPING MENTAL MATH

Many computations with two-digit numbers, fractions, and decimals can be done more efficiently without paper or a calculator. We can help our students develop their mental math skills and assist them in determining when their mind is the best computation tool.

Number Partners

Number Partners develops our students' number sense. In this activity, a set of about ten numbers is written on the board. Students are then asked to find partners (number pairs) that are equivalent to a particular amount (e.g., Find number partners for 250—two numbers that have a sum of 250). Initially numbers such as 10, 25, 50, or 100 provide benchmarks, but with experience, students can find partners that equal

Connections
to other practice standards

Students construct arguments for why certain numbers are mathematical partners (Standard 3).

Students may benefit from the use of models to find number partners (Standard 4).

Number Partners develops students' reasoning about numbers and operations (Standard 2).

250, 500, or 1,000 and explore numbers such as 42, 73, or 88. Students might be challenged with fractions or decimals. Some possibilities include:

Box A: Find Number Partners That Make 10

5	4	9	3	6	1	7	2	5	8

Box B: Find Number Partners That Make 100

25	15	60	35	75	40	90	65	85	10

Box C: Find Number Partners That Make 1,000

250	150	600	350	750	400	900	650	850	100

Box D: Find Number Partners That Make 1

.25	.15	.60	.35	.75	.40	.90	.65	.85	.10

There are countless modifications for this task to increase or decrease the complexity. To simplify the task, we might ask students to identify just one set of number partners or put fewer numbers in the box. To increase the complexity, we might include numbers that don't have partners or ask students to create their own number sets and target numbers that can be posed to the class. This task focuses students on looking for numbers that can be easily combined, giving them practice with mental math and providing insight into the efficiency of mental math.

In My Head?

The *In My Head?* technique develops computational fluency and mental math skills. Students are presented with a handful of problems. Before solving, they decide if the calculation should be done in their head, on paper, or with a calculator. After deciding, students find solutions to the problems. The class then reconvenes to discuss whether they solved the problem mentally or with a tool and why they chose that method.

Connections
to other practice standards

Considering each expression and matching it to the most appropriate tool is a problem-solving experience (Standard 1).

Students construct arguments for why they chose a calculator, paper/pencil, or mental math (Standard 3).

In a third-grade class, we might pose these problems:

$$346 + 99 \qquad 711 - 498 \qquad 149 + 350 \qquad 601 - 598$$

Students may say 346 + 99 is easy to do in their heads by adding 100 and taking 1 away. 711 – 498 may be easier done on paper, although some students may think, "500 less than 711 is 211, and 2 more makes 213." 149 + 350 may yield mixed opinions as well. Students may see it as 100 + 300 + 50 + 49, which is manageable. It is easy to see the difference of 601 and 598 as 3, yet some students believe these large numbers need an algorithm and regrouping.

In a fifth-grade class, we might pose these problems:

$$734 \times 82 \qquad 63 \times 4 \qquad \tfrac{1}{4} + \tfrac{2}{8} \qquad 930 \div 3$$

Students will most likely identify 734×82 as a computation better left to paper or a calculator. 63×4 may be thought too difficult for mental math, but some students may argue it can be done easily when thought of as $(60 \times 4) + (3 \times 4)$. $\tfrac{1}{4} + \tfrac{2}{8}$ will likely show differing opinions as well, with some students making equivalent fractions in their heads and others relying on algorithms. And students may be eager to turn 930 ÷ 3 into a long division algorithm, but students who have developed mental math skills break it apart and state that there are 3 groups of 300, and 3 groups of 10, or 310.

In a seventh-grade class, we might pose:

$$20\% \text{ of } 50 \qquad 132 \div 12 \qquad 1.45 + 13.5 \qquad 17\% \text{ of } 61$$

Some students may be quick to say that all of these are better done with paper and pencil or a calculator, but a few can be easily done mentally. If we know that 20% is the same as $\tfrac{1}{5}$, we can think of the first problem as $\tfrac{1}{5}$ of 50, or 10. 132 ÷ 12 may seem daunting, but if we know 10 groups of 12 are 120, we will quickly notice that 132 is 12 more, or one more group of 12. So 132 ÷ 12 is 11. 1.45 + 13.5 is easier if we break the numbers into wholes and decimal parts. If so, it becomes a simple 1 + 13 and 0.45 + 0.5. The last expression, 17% of 61 IS better solved with a tool of some sort!

It is critical that students share strategies and decisions through class discussion, being sure to acknowledge varied approaches and avoid criticizing those who choose traditional methods. For some students, this may be the first time they have been invited to make decisions on how they will evaluate each expression. Many will automatically pick up their pencil and do what they believe we want them to do—solve it on paper. Our goal is for our students to identify tools that increase *their* efficiency with math tasks.

Give It a Try!

How would your students solve these expressions? Would they choose a calculator, paper and pencil, or mental math? Which would be most efficient? Can they defend their choice?

Primary Expressions	Intermediate Expressions	Middle Grade Expressions
$7 + 4$	14×78	3.508×17.338
$18 + 3$	$909 \div 3$	$13.77 - 12.64$
$77 + 25$	$1{,}250 - 750$	4.5×12
$46 + 37$	$8 \times \frac{3}{4}$	20% of 84
$104 - 12$	$\frac{7}{8} + \frac{3}{9}$	40% of 78

ADDITIONAL IDEAS FOR DEVELOPING THE PRACTICE

What types of tools are available in your math classroom? Do students have opportunities to use tools to explore math tasks? Do you discuss how to use tools and the common errors that occur when using them? Expand on what you are already doing with some of the suggestions below.

Our students are better able to . . .	Because as teachers we . . .
Effectively use tools when solving a mathematical problem.	Model the use of tools as we solve problems (e.g., use grid paper to determine areas of figures, use a ruler to find measures of length, use a calculator to determine products for complex calculations). Make tools available during instruction. Provide opportunities for students to practice with tools. Discuss ways in which tools help simplify the problem-solving process. Ask students which tools might be helpful to solve specific problems.

Our students are better able to . . .	Because as teachers we . . .
Make sound decisions about when certain tools might be helpful, recognizing both their advantages and limitations.	Familiarize our students with a variety of tools. Discuss why we select certain tools. Ask students to identify tools that make sense to solve a problem. Discuss the advantages and limitations of specific tools.
Detect possible errors by strategically using estimation and other mathematical knowledge.	Ask students to estimate prior to using tools and then use their estimate to check for reasonableness. Discuss common errors (e.g., how to know which measure makes sense when using a protractor to measure an angle).
Use technological tools to explore and deepen their understanding of concepts, and recognize that technology can enable them to visualize and analyze math data.	Provide consistent exposure to technology tools (e.g., virtual manipulatives for students at all levels, graphic calculators and dynamic geometry software for middle grades students). Include technology tools during instruction. Discuss potential insights gained from technology tools.

ASSESSMENT TIP

In order to assess students' accuracy with using tools, we might pose tasks that require students to demonstrate their skills (see Figure 6.5). Students might be asked to measure objects or pictures with linking cubes or rulers, to use protractors to determine and record accurate measures of angles, to determine accurate weights using balance scales, or to share their results on a graphing calculator.

To assess students' selection of tools, however, students must be asked to justify their decisions. Writing tasks, like the one in Figure 6.6, share insights into our students' reasoning as they select tools. This student explains why choosing a tape measure would make sense

Figure 6.5 *This student uses a protractor to find the angle measurements of a triangle.*

Figure 6.6 *This student justifies the tool she would choose to measure the board at the front of the classroom.*

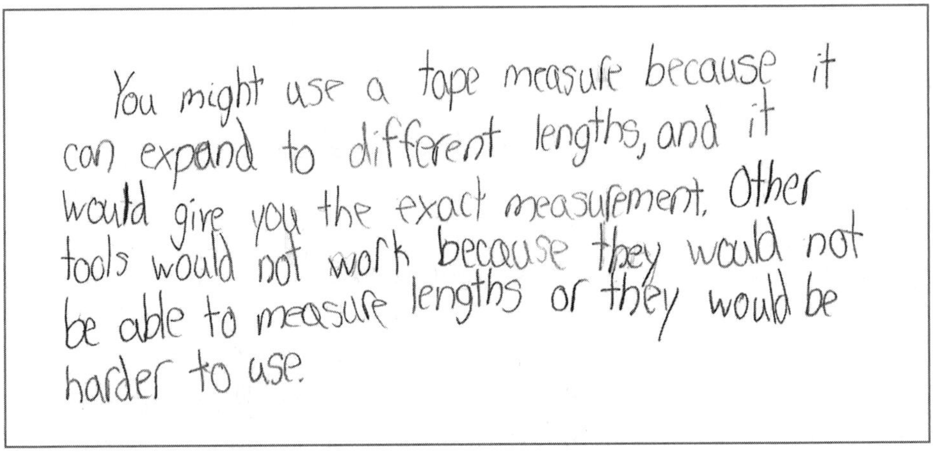

> You might use a tape measure because it can expand to different lengths, and it would give you the exact measurement. Other tools would not work because they would not be able to measure lengths or they would be harder to use.

for measuring the board at the front of the classroom. The teacher might probe for more details about the tools that "would not work" (e.g., a scale or a measuring cup) or why other tools might be "harder to use" (e.g., a ruler or a yardstick).

SUMMING IT UP

The ability to select and use mathematical tools is essential for our students' success in mathematics. While there are many tools that support our students as they perform math tasks, our goal is to help them determine which tools are most efficient for specific tasks. In addition, our students benefit from instruction and practice in the accurate use of a variety of math tools.

Exploring Standard 6: *Attend to Precision*

WHY FOCUS ON PRECISION?

It is true that we often estimate quantities in our daily lives. We add a bit of salt to our recipe instead of measuring exactly $\frac{1}{8}$ teaspoon. We give the waitress a $3.00 tip rather than calculating it exactly. We run *about* a mile rather than mapping out an exact mile-long course. But we also recognize that there are many math tasks that must be exact. We check and recheck our calculations when figuring out our income taxes, and we expect our paychecks to be accurate, reflecting the exact hours worked and our exact pay rate. We make sure our measurements are exact when we want to order window blinds to fit inside a window frame, and we are careful to be precise about those measurements and units when we are placing our order. We calculate with exactness and communicate our math ideas with precision. Math relies on precision, both in computation and in communication.

UNDERSTANDING THE STANDARD

Along with developing an understanding of a diverse range of math skills and concepts, we expect our students to learn basic facts and algorithms so they are able to perform them with precision. We have always emphasized accuracy in math computation, but we also expect accuracy in other math tasks, such as constructing graphs, measuring angles, and determining the probability of events. And along with precision in their computations and procedures, we expect our students to communicate precisely as they describe their math ideas and explain their math thinking. By using the words and symbols of math, our students are able to effectively describe math concepts, explain math procedures, and construct math arguments.

Mathematically proficient students:

▸ calculate accurately and perform math tasks with precision.

▸ communicate precisely.

PRECISION IN CALCULATIONS AND PERFORMING MATH TASKS

We expect our students to be able to calculate exact answers. Initially, precision may be answers expressed in whole numbers, but as our students progress in their skills, that precision is refined with answers expressed as decimals to the tenths, hundredths, or thousandths. Through teacher modeling, exploration of algorithms, and guided practice, our students work toward precision. And, just as important, they begin to develop an understanding of the value of precision. They identify when estimates make sense and when exactness is preferred. They use estimates as benchmarks to check the reasonableness of their answers and check for accuracy using their knowledge of inverse operations (e.g., if we calculated that $321 - 117 = 204$, then $204 + 117$ must equal 321) or properties (e.g., the distributive property helps us verify that $54 \times 8 = 432$, since $50 \times 8 = 400$, and $4 \times 8 = 32$, so 432 is correct!).

But precision is not just for computations. Accurate measurement relies on precision. As primary students line up cubes to measure an object, we often notice gaps between the cubes. As they develop their skills, attention is placed on moving the cubes together to eliminate gaps and the measurements become more precise. Rulers, with markings for each inch, replace the cubes and increase precision. Later, the markings on the ruler become even more precise as our students measure to the eighth or sixteenth of an inch.

Probability investigations initially yield insights that events are more or less likely than others. Then, with the expectation of greater precision, the likelihood of events is described with fractions and decimals (e.g., a 65% chance of selecting a yellow cube from a bag). Mathematicians strive to be precise.

PRECISION IN COMMUNICATION

Mathematicians communicate precisely. We expect our students to use words or symbols to label quantities so they are more specific—4 girls, 13 inches, 52 tens, $35.17, or 76%. We expect them to thoroughly describe math ideas, precisely explain how they solve a problem, and give specific examples as they construct mathematical arguments. Throughout the Practices, we have stressed the importance of math discussion, but how effective will our students be if they do not have a strong understanding of the language of math? Finding just the right word, or using just the right symbol, to express their ideas allows our students to communicate effectively about math. Developing familiarity with the language of math provides them with the tools to communicate with precision.

Communicating Through Words

Talking and writing about math allows our students to share their ideas and allows us to gain insights into their thinking—but only if we can understand what they are saying. It may not come naturally for our students to talk and write about math, and the inability to find the right words to express their ideas can contribute to the difficulty of this task. Math is filled with words that are hard for our students to understand. They are bombarded with technical words such as *sum, vertices, parallel, factors, ratio,* and *variables*. They are confused by everyday words that have different meanings in math class such as *feet, faces, power,* and *volume*. They struggle to remember the specific words that connect to math concepts, and without proper word choice their communication becomes confusing and inaccurate.

Chrissy shared that she "timesed it," rather than explaining that she multiplied 3 bags by 4 candies in each bag. Kari contended that she measured "around it," rather than talking about the perimeter of the figure. Jack described how he measured the angles of a triangle by "putting it on and then looking at the numbers and then saw it was 25." Does he mean that he placed the *protractor* on the *ray* and looked at the measurements to find the angle measurement of 25 *degrees*? To communicate effectively about math content, our students need to know the words that express that content. When their language is clear and precise, their ideas become understandable.

A focus on the meaning of critical vocabulary should be an integral part of our content instruction. Our students are best introduced to new words through familiar language, synonyms, examples, and pictures to help them gain a clear understanding of both the math concepts and the math language. Students increase their facility with math vocabulary through opportunities to talk with others, helping them become more familiar with the words as they experiment with using them to express their ideas. And through ongoing opportunities to talk and write about their thinking, students become more skilled at selecting the precise words to express their ideas.

2.G.1

Mrs. Alexander asked her second graders to draw a rectangle on their papers. She asked them to turn to a partner and check each other's drawings.

> **Teacher:** How can you prove that is a rectangle?
>
> **Bobby:** It looks like a rectangle.
>
> **Teacher:** What do you mean?
>
> **Ellen:** It's shaped like a rectangle—like that sign on the wall.
>
> **Teacher:** But what makes that sign a rectangle?
>
> **Billy:** It is flat and has 4 sides and 4 corners.
>
> **Teacher:** So, if a shape is flat and has 4 sides and 4 corners (we call them *vertices*) it's a rectangle? Talk to your partner. Is that always true?

Students talked with partners and then Mrs. Alexander continued the class discussion.

> **Mary:** No, some aren't. Like a trapezoid has 4 sides and 4 corners, but it's not a rectangle.
>
> **Teacher:** Why not? Why is your drawing a rectangle, but a trapezoid is not a rectangle? They both have 4 sides and 4 vertices and they are both flat.
>
> **Alice:** The sides aren't straight on a trapezoid.
>
> **Teacher:** What do you mean they aren't straight?
>
> **James:** They don't both stay straight. One comes in closer.
>
> **Teacher:** Does anyone remember what we call those lines?
>
> **Alice:** Parallel.
>
> **Teacher:** Nice word, Alice.

Mrs. Alexander wrote the word *parallel* on the board and drew 2 parallel lines.

> **Teacher:** What is special about these lines? Does anyone remember?
>
> **James:** They don't get closer together.

Drew: Like if you measured them, they wouldn't be closer together.

Teacher: So, what about a rectangle? Do the sides get closer together?

Charles: No, and the vertices are different, too. They are right angles.

Teacher: What do you mean? Tell me more about the vertices.

Charles: All 4 vertices are right angles—like on a square.

Teacher: Can you show us what the right angles look like?

Charles went to the board and drew a rectangle and showed the 4 right angles.

Teacher: Do all of your rectangles have right angles? Talk with your partners.

> Notice that throughout this discussion the teacher is reinforcing math vocabulary and teaching geometry concepts simultaneously.

Mrs. Alexander led the students in summing up their ideas about rectangles, composing a class definition.

A rectangle is a flat shape.

It has 4 sides and 4 vertices.

The vertices are right angles.

The opposite sides are parallel.

Mrs. Alexander drew some rectangles of different sizes and in different orientations on the board and asked the students to tell her if they were rectangles, based on their definition. She had the class brainstorm examples of real-world rectangles. She then added the words *rectangle, right angle,* and *parallel* to the math word wall and included a drawing to illustrate each new word. Through the class discussion, Mrs. Alexander had assisted students in developing the definition of a rectangle, and while doing so had paused to clarify other math terms (*right angle* and *parallel*). She used pictures and examples to build understanding and helped her students refine their words to craft a more precise definition of a rectangle. She ended by having each of her students create a page for a class book about rectangles, asking them to show what they knew about a rectangle with words, pictures, and examples.

In order to communicate precisely, our students must both understand the math and know the words that express that understanding. Mr. Brett's fourth graders were asked to define a numerator to their partners. As Mr. Brett walked through the room, the majority of his students simply verbalized that it was the number on the top in a fraction. "But what *is* a numerator?" he restated. Their confused looks showed that they could not explain what the number represented and hoped that their superficial response would be accepted as the definition. Mr. Griffin asked his sixth graders to describe *surface area* and Jonah answered, "It's the outside of something." And in Mrs. Farrington's eighth-grade class, students were asked to define a variable. "It's the *n*," Mary said, confident that she was correct. When our students' definitions lack specificity we rightfully question the depth of their understanding.

Communicating with Symbols

Math is a language filled with symbols. Numerals represent quantities. The equal sign represents equality. We record > or < to compare quantities that are not equal. A number with $ before it represents dollars, and the number with ¢ behind it represents cents. Our students must be able to decode symbols in order to understand math ideas (e.g., 4^3 is the same as $4 \times 4 \times 4$). And our students must also be able to encode ideas in symbols to convey their understanding in writing (e.g., if 12 counters is more than 8 counters, students write $12 > 8$).

But understanding symbols is more than the ability to read them. Mrs. Cooley posed this equation to her third-grade class and asked her students to talk with partners to decide how they would complete it.

$$6 \times 4 = \underline{\quad} \times 3$$

Janie contended, "It doesn't make sense. It should just have a blank, not a number, too." While Julie confidently filled in the blank with "24 because $6 \times 4 = 24$." Mrs. Cooley's students knew the name for the equal sign, but they were not clear on its meaning. Their responses indicated misunderstandings about the concept of equality. Being able to name a symbol does not ensure that our students understand the meaning of that symbol.

Specifying units or labels adds to the precision of math communication. When determining perimeter, area, and volume, answers are reported as units, units^2, or units^3. But do our students know what the superscript "2" represents? Do they connect it to the concept of multiplication? Computationally fluent middle school students may know the symbol for percent, but can they explain what 33% of 75 means? Students must be able to use and explain the symbols of math. For that to happen, we must be comfortable and intentional when using symbols in the math classroom, consistently checking to be sure our students know their meaning and how to use them.

We expect precision from our students from labeling the units used (e.g., inches, feet, centimeters) to identifying what the quantity represents in problem-solving situations (e.g., 8 boys, 8 crayons, 8 inches, $8.00, 8%). Labeling, whether in words or symbols, adds to the precision of mathematics.

HOW DO WE GET THERE?

What can we do to help our students develop precision? What strategies, activities, and discussions would enhance what is happening in our classrooms? How do we help our students become precise in their computations and communication?

CLASSROOM-TESTED TECHNIQUES

ESTIMATE AND EXACT   Helping our students compute precisely is important, but so is helping them determine *when* precision is necessary. Pose situations in which students must decide whether an estimate or an exact answer is needed. Allow for discussions so students are able to back up their decisions with reasoning.

> **Buying bags of candy to put in party treat bags**
>
> **Buying pizzas for a class party**
>
> **Measuring the dimensions of the doorway to install a screen door**
>
> **Buying carpeting for a living room floor**

Have students work with partners to develop arguments for whether an exact or an estimated answer makes more sense in each situation.

Estimation also helps us determine if our answers are reasonable, which in turn aids our precision. Frequently ask students to estimate sums and differences, quotients and products, equivalencies and percentages, before finding exact answers, then have students refer back to their estimates to check the reasonableness of their exact computations. Doing so helps students improve their number sense, computation, and precision.

In our classrooms, we might practice estimation skills with prompts like the following:

> *Will the sum of 8 + 7 be greater than or less than 20? Why?*
>
> *Is the difference of 81 and 29 closer to 40, 50, or 60? Why?*
>
> *What might the quotient of 239 ÷ 4 be? Explain your thinking.*
>
> *Is the sum of $\frac{1}{3} + \frac{4}{8}$ greater than or less than 2? Why?*
>
> *How would you estimate the product of 2.4 and 63? Will the product be between 2 × 60 and 3 × 60? Why or why not?*
>
> *How do we know if 23% of 82 is close to 20?*

Connections
to other practice standards

Estimate and Exact provides opportunities for students to argue why their approach is appropriate (Standard 3).

Estimate and Exact urges students to generalize about mathematics (e.g., The product of 5.3 and 38 will be close to 200 because 5 x 40 is 200) (Standard 8).

VOCABULARY

In order for our students to internalize the language of math, they need repeated and meaningful opportunities to explore math words. These opportunities are integrated with content teaching and help our students develop vocabulary while they also extend our students' content knowledge.

Connections
to other practice standards

Students justify how their words are related to the word that is being webbed (Standard 3).

WORD WEBS   *Word Webs* are a quick and effective way to explore math ideas and expand math vocabulary. Pose a word to your students, and have them turn to a partner or small group and share some related words. Have students jot the related words on their word web in preparation for class discussion. (Kindergarten students simply share the words orally.)

Mrs. Robinson wrote the term *equally likely* on the board, and students began to share and record words that related to the term. Once students had a few minutes to generate related words, Mrs. Robinson began a discussion, asking groups to share some of their words. As they shared, she posed questions to prompt discussions about the words and their meanings.

> **Teacher:** What did you think of when I said *equally likely*?
>
> **Brooks:** We said *chance*.
>
> **Mary:** We said *equal chance*.
>
> **Teacher:** Why? How is *chance* related to *equally likely*?
>
> **Mary:** 'Cause *likely* is when it could happen, like a *chance* and it is equal.
>
> **Teacher:** What do you mean the *chance* is *equal*? Can anyone give an example of something that is *equally likely*?
>
> **Emma:** When you flip a coin. Same chance of getting heads or tails.
>
> **Olivia:** Or if you roll a die you have the same chance of getting 1, 2, 3, 4, 5, or 6.
>
> **Teacher:** Have we done anything in class where the outcomes were *equally likely*?
>
> **Josh:** When we pulled red and blue cubes from the bag last week. It was *equally likely*.
>
> **Teacher:** Why?

Josh: We had the same number of red and blue cubes in the bag. We had the same *chance* of getting red or blue.

Teacher: What other words did you think of when I said *equally likely*?

The discussion continued with words like *outcomes*, *events*, *probability*, *percent*, and *fraction*, with the teacher simply asking questions and informally discussing the related words and concepts. Struggling students had an opportunity to hear the words and meanings through familiar language, examples, and synonyms. Students who already knew the words were challenged to describe and explain them.

Give It a Try!

Select a term that relates to your content standards (e.g., *square* for kindergarten, *denominator* for fourth grade, or *compound events* for eighth grade). Following students' brainstorming of related words, facilitate a discussion using familiar language, drawing pictures, and stimulating thought through questions like the following:

Why did you think of that word?

How does it relate to our word of the day?

What is _____?

Can you give me an example of _____?

When have we talked about _____ before?

Even if your students' words do not correctly match the word of the day (e.g., for *square*, students said *box*), we are able to correct misunderstandings (e.g., one side of a box can be a square), rephrase ideas, and clarify the word's meaning. Through discussions of related words, we are able to quickly explore word meanings.

WORD WALLS Classroom *Word Walls* highlight key vocabulary and are beneficial in math classrooms K–8. By placing the content vocabulary in a prominent location in the classroom, students are able to quickly access key words as they are talking or writing about math ideas.

Word walls are instructional tools that are built with students. Simply writing a word on a sentence strip at the point of exposure to the word—and including a diagram or an example to illustrate its meaning—allows our students to focus on the word during instruction and refer back to the word as needed while they are becoming more familiar with its use. And classroom word walls create opportunities for quick vocabulary review as teachers give a clue for students to find the word (e.g., I am a polygon with 5 sides and 5 vertices) or ask students to develop arguments as to why two words belong together (e.g., square and rhombus or ratio and fraction).

SORT AND LABEL   Through word sorts, students identify similarities and differences between math concepts as they explore the list of words. How would your students sort and label the following lists?

> *sum, minus, join, compare, subtract, add, take apart, plus*
>
> *pint, foot, measuring cup, ounce, inch, scale, yard, pound, quart, ruler*
>
> *square, trapezoid, hexagon, rectangle, rhombus, triangle, pentagon*
>
> *surface area, cm³, volume, perimeter, cm, area, cm², length,*
>
> *expression, equation, addition, operation, inequality, comparison, variable, division*

As students sort these math words with partners, they discuss the concepts represented by the words (see Figure 7.1). They look for subtleties in the meanings of the words in order to sort and classify them. Can *ounce* go with *pound*, or should we put it with capacity words (e.g., *fluid ounce*)? Could we justify either? Should we make a category for *quadrilaterals*, and if so, which polygons would work with that classification (Square? Trapezoid? Rectangle? Rhombus?)? But if we classify them as *parallelograms*, which polygons would fit? Is there only one way to sort each set of words? Can students develop arguments to justify their sorting? Would the sorting of these words strengthen students' content understanding? Would it help them become more familiar with the language? Through active engagement and ongoing discussion, *Sort and Label* tasks build our students' content understanding and expand their familiarity with math words.

Figure 7.1   *These students discuss and sort math words into categories that make sense based on the meanings of the words.*

MYSTERY WORDS   Can your students verbalize the meanings of math words? Give each pair of students a set of word cards and have partners take turns picking a card at random. Can students describe the mystery word, without actually saying the word? Can their partners listen to the clues and figure out the mystery word? They must continue to give clues until the word is identified.

TRANSLATE THE SYMBOL Can your students represent math ideas with numbers and symbols? How might they represent the following math ideas?

4 dollars and 10 cents is greater than 4 dollars and 5 cents	$\$4.10 > \$4.05$
One-fourth of 16 is 4	$\frac{1}{4}(16) = 4$
Doubling a number then adding 6 more	$2n + 6$

The ability to use symbols to represent math ideas is an important skill, but can students explain symbols in ways that show that they fully understand what the symbols represent?

Place math expressions, equations, or inequalities on index cards and have students select a card and explain it to their partner, or explain it in writing. Some possibilities might include:

$12 = 7 + 5$	6^3
$4 > 2$	$m \angle B = 45°$
$25¢$	1.83×10^3
$3 \times 4 > 2 \times 5$	$4 + x = -6$
45%	

Connections
to other practice standards

Translate the Symbol naturally connects with decontextualizing skills (Standard 2).

Students must use their understanding of symbols to argue the meaning of expressions or equations (Standard 3).

TIPS FOR WRITING ABOUT MATH

▶ While knowing the words of mathematics contributes to our students' abilities to precisely communicate their ideas, being able to formulate clear explanations requires more than a grasp of math vocabulary. Our students are asked to explain how they solved problems, justify solutions, and describe math concepts. Consider the following tips to help students more effectively talk and write about their math ideas:

▸ When students are asked to explain a process (e.g., how they solved a problem or performed a complex calculation), steps and order are key elements. Writing their ideas in a numbered list simplifies the task for students as it helps them organize and clearly communicate the steps of the process.

(continues)

▶ When asked to justify an answer, expect students to provide the solution and data or reasoning that defends that solution. Have students think about a *because* statement, "The solution is ___ *because*. . . ." Thinking about a *because* statement reminds them that proof for their solution is an integral part of your expectation.

▶ When describing math concepts (e.g., congruent, symmetry, multiple, factorial, exponent, etc.), the brief responses we tend to get from students lack the detail necessary to adequately describe the concept. Remind students to use words, pictures, numbers, and examples to provide additional elaboration.

For more tips on strengthening students' writing about math, see *Introduction to Communication* (O'Connell 2007a).

ADDITIONAL IDEAS FOR DEVELOPING THE PRACTICE

How precise are our students? Do they calculate with accuracy? Are they exact in their labeling of problem data and answers? Are they able to talk about their math ideas using the language of mathematics? Do you see precision as they write about their strategies and justify their solutions? Expand on what you are already doing with some of the suggestions below.

Our students are better able to . . .	Because as teachers we . . .
Communicate precisely using clear definitions.	Model precise communication by using grade-level-appropriate vocabulary.
	Discuss important math vocabulary and explore the meanings of math words through familiar language, words, pictures, and examples.
	Expect precise communication and ask students to elaborate on ideas, choose specific words, specify units, and explain symbols.
	Orchestrate ongoing opportunities for students to talk and write about math.

Our students are better able to . . .	Because as teachers we . . .
State the meaning of the symbols they choose.	Discuss and consistently ask our students to explain the meaning of symbols (=, <, >). Explore varied ways in which symbols might be presented (e.g., $5 \times 3 = 15$ and $15 = 3 \times 5$).
Specify units of measure, and label axes to clarify the correspondence with quantities in a problem.	Ask students to label units, quantities, and graphs. Expect students to justify labels (e.g., why *area* is labeled as square units and *volume* is labeled as cubic units).
Calculate accurately and efficiently and express numerical answers with a degree of precision appropriate for the problem context.	Expect accuracy, except in cases in which we have asked for estimates or where estimates make more sense. Expect precision as appropriate for the grade-level and content expectations (e.g., $\frac{1}{4}$ inch vs. $\frac{3}{16}$ inch; 5 vs. 5.2 or 5.24).
Formulate explanations to each other.	Model specific and thorough explanations. Discuss our expectations and offer tips for formulating clear explanations (see highlighted box). Allow students opportunities to work with partners to formulate explanations.

ASSESSMENT TIP

We certainly want to avoid asking our students to copy dictionary definitions as a classroom or homework task. Our students copy definitions without ever thinking about, or understanding, the words they are copying. The activities mentioned earlier in this chapter focus on our students building understanding of math vocabulary, so a natural assessment would be to ask students to describe or define math terms. Earlier in this chapter we discussed second graders' descriptions of a rectangle, with some being very broad and nonspecific and finally becoming specific and detailed. The detailed definition demonstrated an understanding of a rectangle, while "It's a shape" did not. Can students thoroughly answer these questions?

▸ What is a triangle?
▸ What is a sum?

▶ What are parallel lines?

▶ What is a denominator?

▶ What is a right angle?

▶ What is a hundredth?

▶ What is a variable?

▶ What are independent events?

Ask students to explain a math term in their own words. Remind them that they can show what they know through words, pictures, numbers, and examples. The format of the word box works as well for assessment as it does for instruction, reminding students to define a word thoroughly as they complete each section (Figures 7.2 and 7.3). Asking students to construct their own definitions allows us to truly see what they know.

Figure 7.2   *This student shares her understanding of symmetry through definitions, examples, pictures, and related words.*

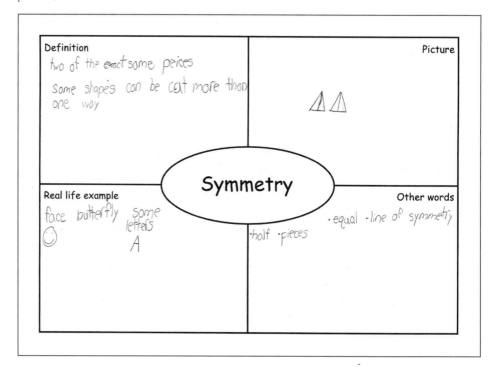

Figure 7.3 *At all grade levels, word boxes allow us to assess our students' understanding of math words and concepts.*

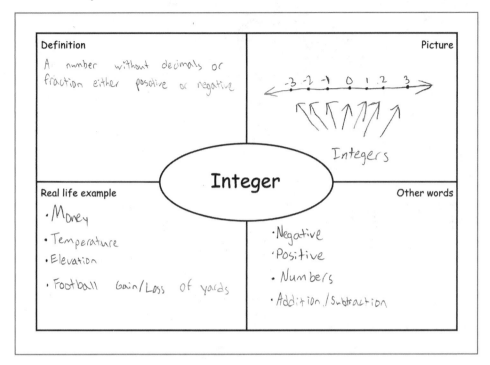

Definition	Picture
A number without decimals or fraction either positive or negative	Integers

Integer

Real life example	Other words
• Money	• Negative
• Temperature	• Positive
• Elevation	• Numbers
• Football Gain/Loss of yards	• Addition./Subtraction

SUMMING IT UP

Mathematicians are precise in both their calculations and in their communication. To be precise in calculations, our students must be skilled at algorithms or other math skills, such as measurement, geometric reasoning, or probability. To be precise in communication, our students must understand and be able to use the words and symbols of math. Familiarity with the language of math allows them to construct strong responses, precisely explain their problem-solving strategies, and explicitly describe math concepts.

Exploring Standard 7:
Look for and Make Use of Structure

WHY FOCUS ON STRUCTURE?

Many people see math as confusing, not always sure how the answers are achieved. Math, however, is quite predictable. There is structure in math, and people who see that structure find that math makes sense. When we add our monthly bills, we don't worry about the order in which we add them. If we understand the way math works (math properties), we know that the order in which the numbers are added will never change the total. We look for patterns to understand rising prices or stock market changes. We break apart numbers as needed to perform tasks (e.g., when we can't find the $\frac{3}{4}$ measuring cup, we simply measure $\frac{1}{4}$ cup of flour three times, knowing it is the same quantity). We apply what we know about the structure of math—its patterns and properties—as we use math each day.

UNDERSTANDING THE STANDARD

This standard focuses on understanding the structure of mathematics. Patterns and functions are everywhere. Properties guide us as we explore and simplify math computations. If our students understand the structure of mathematics, they will find that math makes sense.

Numbers are flexible. They can be broken apart and put together. Seven can be broken into 4 + 3; 4 and 3 can be joined to make 7. When we compare 9 and 12, the difference is always 3, because 9 + 3 = 12. 6 × 8 is the same as 5 × 8 plus 1 × 8. 6 × 8 is the same as 6 × 4 plus 6 × 4. 3(*n* + 2) is the same as (3 × *n*) + (3 × 2), or 3*n* + 6. Breaking numbers apart and putting them together is a regular part of doing mathematics.

Our number system is a system of patterns. Everywhere we turn in mathematics, patterns are evident. Ten ones make a 10 and 10 tens make 100, and so on, as we explore place value. Not surprisingly, 10 hundredths make a tenth and 10 tenths make a whole. Our place-value system is based on patterns. We mentioned that 7 could be broken into 4 + 3, but 7 can also be broken into 5 + 2 or 6 + 1 or 7 + 0. What an interesting pattern—one addend increases while the other decreases!

Patterns abound in higher mathematics as well. Have your students noticed the patterns within fractions and decimals? When we halve a fraction, its decimal equivalent is also halved. Knowledge of benchmark equivalencies ($\frac{1}{2}$ = .50) helps our students determine equivalent decimals (see Figure 8.1). If we don't immediately know the decimal representation of $\frac{3}{8}$, but we know that $\frac{1}{4}$ is .25 and that $\frac{1}{8}$ is half of that or .125, we can triple .125 to find that $\frac{3}{8}$ is .375.

Properties show the structure of math as we explore the relationships between (2 + 7) + 1 and 7 + (2 + 1) or 3 × 5 and 5 × 3. Once we understand that order doesn't change the sum or product, our computations are simplified. Identity properties help us make sense of 5 + 0 = 5 or 4 × 1 = 4, and the distributive property makes numbers easier to work with since breaking them apart does not change them, much as 7 × 5 is the same as (5 × 5) + (2 × 5). When our students understand the commutative property and the way numbers can be decomposed, fact families make sense (4 × 5 = 20, 5 × 4 = 20, 20 ÷ 4 = 5, and 20 ÷ 5 = 4).

Mathematically proficient students:

▸ see the flexibility of numbers.

▸ understand properties.

▸ recognize patterns and functions.

Figure 8.1 *Do your students see the patterns in these fraction/decimal equivalents?*

$\frac{1}{2}$ = .50	$\frac{1}{3}$ = .33	$\frac{1}{5}$ = .20
$\frac{1}{4}$ = .25	$\frac{1}{6}$ = .167	$\frac{1}{10}$ = .10
$\frac{1}{8}$ = .125	$\frac{1}{12}$ = .083	$\frac{1}{20}$ = .05
$\frac{1}{16}$ = .0625	$\frac{1}{24}$ = .0467	$\frac{1}{40}$ = .025

THE FLEXIBILITY OF NUMBERS

Numbers can be composed (put together) and decomposed (broken apart). Mrs. King gave her kindergarten students 5 two-color counters and had them shake and then spill the counters from a cup to find different ways they could make 5. Each time the counters spilled, the students counted the number that were red, the number that were yellow, and the total. Her students noticed that the 5 counters might be 5 red and 0 yellow, or 4 red and 1 yellow, or 3 red and 2 yellow, but the total was always 5. Mrs. King's students were exploring the flexibility of numbers.

Mrs. O'Connor posed the following problem to her fourth-grade students.

> *There was $1\frac{1}{2}$ cupcakes left on the plate and Liam and Molly decided they would eat them. How much might each person have eaten? Be ready to justify your answers.*

Some of her students used fraction templates while others drew diagrams to find different ways to break apart $1\frac{1}{2}$. While many started with the obvious: 1 for one person and $\frac{1}{2}$ for the other, they soon realized that there were many options for sharing the $1\frac{1}{2}$ cupcake. Blake showed a drawing of $1\frac{1}{4}$ and $\frac{1}{4}$ to justify her solution, while Colin suggested that, "$\frac{3}{4}$ and $\frac{3}{4}$ would work because $\frac{3}{4}$ would leave $\frac{1}{4}$ more, and if you put that with the $\frac{1}{2}$ it would be another $\frac{3}{4}$." Bailey split the whole cupcake into sixths, determining that there would be "three parts in the half." She then suggested they could share $\frac{5}{6}$ and $\frac{4}{6}$, using fraction pieces (manipulatives) to convince the class of the accuracy of her solution. The students were deepening their understanding of fractions as they decomposed $1\frac{1}{2}$.

> Notice that the problem had more than one solution, which spurred students to explore and justify their solutions.

DISCOVERING PROPERTIES

Ms. Moran's first graders were exploring the commutative property of addition. Mrs. Moran gave them part-part-whole mats and asked them to show each problem below and then write the number sentence to go with it.

1.OA.1; 1.OA.3

> *Jack had 3 tickets and Jill had 4 tickets. How many tickets did they have altogether? (3 + 4 = 7)*
>
> *Jack had 4 tickets and Jill had 3 tickets. How many tickets did they have altogether? (4 + 3 = 7)*
>
> *There were 6 black dogs and 4 white dogs. How many dogs were there? (6 + 4 = 10)*
>
> *There were 4 black dogs and 6 white dogs. How many dogs were there? (4 + 6 = 10)*

After several examples, Mrs. Moran posed the following problems, asking her students to use their counters to find the first answer and then predict what they thought the next answer would be and be ready to justify their predictions.

> *The vase held 5 red roses and 3 yellow roses. How many roses were in the vase?*
>
> *The vase held 3 red roses and 5 yellow roses. How many roses were in the vase?*

Her students noted that $5 + 3 = 8$ and then Jenna said, "It has to be 8." Joey agreed. "It is the same. It doesn't matter which is red or yellow." Greta chimed in, "All of them are the same. We just wrote a different number first." Mrs. Moran's students were discovering the commutative property.

Mrs. Partin posed the following problem to her third-grade class:

> *The auditorium has 14 rows of seats and 8 seats in every row. How many people can be seated?*

3.OA.3; 3.OA.5

While some students struggled with the complexity of the problem data, Janis immediately broke apart the 14 rows to think about 10 rows plus 4 more rows. She quickly got the answer and explained: "$10 \times 8 = 80$ and $4 \times 8 = 32$ and $80 + 32 = 112$. It was easier to break it up. I could just do the multiplication in my head. Then all I had to do was add it." Understanding the distributive property helped Janis simplify the task.

RECOGNIZING PATTERNS AND FUNCTIONS

Mr. Kindle began an exploration with his first-grade class. He asked them to work in partners to solve the following problem. Students were given counters and paper to record their possibilities. Mr. Kindle acknowledged that there could be more than one answer to his problem and challenged students to find as many answers as they could.

> *There were 10 children at the party. How many were boys and how many were girls?*

1.OA.1; 1.OA.3; 1.OA.6

As his students explored the task, they grabbed counters and began to model the problem. They recorded possibilities as they found them and then continued working to find other possibilities. Once students had generated lots of possibilities, Mr. Kindle had them share their possibilities as he recorded them on the board. For each possibility, he asked if others had gotten it too, and if they hadn't, he asked them to check with their counters to verify its correctness. He asked students to talk with partners about their observations and found that students noticed the following:

"The numbers can be switched. We had 3 + 7 and 7 + 3."

"Yeah—we had 4 + 6 and 6 + 4."

They explored all of the number combinations to find that every boy/girl combination could be reversed and still total 10 children.

Mr. Kindle then arranged their possibilities in order, beginning with 0 + 10 and ending with 10 + 0, as in Figure 8.2, and asked students to observe the data.

The students noticed the patterns "counting up" and "counting down."

Liam: When boys goes up, girls goes down.

Teacher: Why is that happening?

Kristen: If we put in another girl, we have to take a boy away.

Figure 8.2 *The class data was compiled and students were asked to observe the data.*

BOYS	GIRLS
0	10
1	9
2	8
3	7
4	6
5	5
6	4
7	3
8	2
9	1
10	0

Mr. Kindle suggested that students model the idea on ten-frames.

>   **Teacher:** So, every time we add a girl, we have to take away a boy?

>   **Oscar:** Yes, there is only room for 10.

Mr. Kindle's students were exploring the commutative property, patterns, and the flexibility of numbers as they explored this problem task.

Mrs. Foley's third-grade class created a table to show the number of tickets needed to ride on the carousel at the fair. For each ride, a student needed 3 tickets. Together, they created the following table:

3.OA.9

Number of rides	1	2	3	4	5
Number of tickets	3	6	9	12	15

Kara noticed a pattern in the number of tickets needed for each additional ride as she commented, "It goes 3, 6, 9, 12, 15—you just count by threes." Emma noticed a function, "You just × 3 each time, if you look down, like 2 × 3 is 6 and 3 × 3 is 9." Mrs. Foley's third graders discovered the power of tables as their data table allowed them to see the patterns and functions clearly. Ultimately, the discovery of functions allows students to efficiently solve more complex problems. How many tickets would we need if we rode the carousel 20 times? Rather than continuing the pattern of counting by threes 20 times, students who have discovered the function ($3n$) can simply triple the number of rides ($3 \times 20 = 60$ tickets).

Mrs. Bender showed her sixth-grade students a row of five connected equilateral triangles.

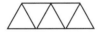

She then posed the following problem:

>   ***If there was a row of 50 connected equilateral triangles,***
>   ***what would the perimeter measure?***

6.EE.9; 6.EE.6

Students worked in pairs to explore the problem. Mrs. Bender asked her students to talk with partners about perimeter, how it is measured, and what unit of measurement would be appropriate. She also reminded them to be ready to justify their answers. Several pairs started drawing connected triangles, but they became frustrated as the row got longer. Steve and Angela found the perimeter for the five connected

Figure 8.3 *By analyzing the data in the table, students were able to identify the function ($n + 2$): the perimeter is always 2 units more than the number of triangles.*

Number of triangles	1	2	3	4	5	6	7	8	9
Perimeter in units	3	4	5	6	7	8	9	10	11

triangles (7 units) and multiplied 7 × 10 = 70 units, since "a row of 50 triangles is 10 times more than a row of 5 triangles."

Eric and Patricia reported that the perimeter would be 52. They explained that they had created a table to show the perimeters as each new triangle was added and shared the pattern that helped them find the answer. Eric explained, "The perimeter started at 3 and then you add one more unit each time you add a triangle, so we counted 49 more times and got to 52."

Janis and Nick agreed that 52 units was the perimeter, but Janis explained, "You just look at the top and bottom numbers. Every time it's 2 more. The perimeter is 2 more than the triangles every time, so we said 50 + 2 is 52 units." Janis and Nick had identified the function (see Figure 8.3) and their solution was both correct and efficient.

HOW DO WE GET THERE?

CLASSROOM-TESTED TECHNIQUES

Exploring Patterns and Functions

PATTERN COVER-UP Ongoing exploration of patterns reminds students that number patterns are everywhere. On the board or chart paper, write a number pattern, covering each number with a sticky note so students cannot see the numbers. Remove one sticky note to reveal a number. Ask students to predict what the covered numbers might be and describe the pattern they suspect is under the sticky notes.

For example:

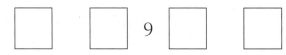

Students might predict 7, 8, 9, 10, 11 or 3, 6, 9, 12, 15 or 2, 5, 9, 14, 20, etc. Have them describe the patterns they predicted (i.e., they might describe 3, 6, 9, 12,

Connections
to other practice standards

Pattern Cover-Up is a natural problem for students to grapple with (Standard 1).

Discussing possible patterns makes use of students' reasoning and their ability to communicate it (Standard 3).

Students may use models, like hundred charts, to explore the patterns (Standard 4).

15 as counting by 3s or adding 3 more each time or increasing by 3). Record their predictions. Then remove another sticky note to reveal another piece of the pattern. Ask students to predict again and describe their new patterns. Can they eliminate any of their previous predictions? Continue removing sticky notes until the pattern is revealed. Patterns can be as simple or as complex as is appropriate for the grade level.

PATTERNS IN THE HUNDRED CHART OR MULTIPLICATION CHART   Hundred charts and multiplication charts are great places to search for patterns. Have students search for patterns, highlight them, and describe their patterns to the class.

▶ On a hundred chart, can students explain the vertical and horizontal pattern? Do they see diagonal patterns?

▶ On a multiplication chart, can students explain vertical and horizontal patterns? Do they see diagonal patterns? Can they find patterns that explore equivalent fractions or proportions (e.g., any two rows as highlighted in Figure 8.4)?

Connections
to other practice standards

Students use a model to represent numbers and identify patterns (Standard 4).

Students use their reasoning and communication skills to precisely describe patterns (Standards 3 and 6).

Figure 8.4   *Looking horizontally across the highlighted rows shows proportions, or equivalent fractions, for $\frac{3}{4}$.*

×	1	2	3	4	5	6	7	8	9	10
1	1	2	3	4	5	6	7	8	9	10
2	2	4	6	8	10	12	14	16	18	20
3	3	6	9	12	15	18	21	24	27	30
4	4	8	12	16	20	24	28	32	36	40
5	5	10	15	20	25	30	35	40	45	50
6	6	12	18	24	30	36	42	48	54	60
7	7	14	21	28	35	42	49	56	63	70
8	8	16	24	32	40	48	56	64	72	80
9	9	18	27	36	45	54	63	72	81	90
10	10	20	30	40	50	60	70	80	90	100

RATIO TABLES TO EXPLORE PATTERNS AND FUNCTIONS   Help your students see the value of ratio tables for solving math problems. Ratio tables make sense when two pieces of data are connected. In the following problem the number of flowers and the number of leaves are connected.

> *Margo was painting flowers on the classroom mural. Every*
> *flower had 3 leaves. How many leaves were on the mural*
> *after 7 flowers had been painted?*

Creating a table to show the relationship between the number of flowers and the number of leaves (Figure 8.5) allows students to clearly see patterns (the number of leaves increasing by 3 with each flower) and functions (the number of leaves is 3 × the number of flowers). Have students look at the data both vertically and horizontally to gain insights about the connections between the data. Ask them to describe the patterns or functions that they see.

Pose problems in which data tables are a reasonable strategy, although not the only strategy, for solving the problems. Have students share their insights after creating and observing their tables.

> *Each chicken has 2 legs. How many legs are on 4 chickens?*
>
> *2 jars of peanut butter cost $4.50. How much do 8 jars cost?*
>
> *To make a cake, Kelly needs 4 eggs. How many eggs are*
> *needed to make 5 cakes?*
>
> *The movie theater was having a special deal—2 admissions*
> *for $12.00. How much did it cost for Kara and her 7 friends*
> *to go to the movies?*
>
> *To make one dozen ice-cream sandwiches, Katie used $\frac{3}{4}$*
> *gallon of ice cream. How much ice cream did she need for*
> *60 ice-cream sandwiches?*

Ratio tables support students as they develop understanding and automaticity with multiplication and division math facts. After building a ×6 table (Figure 8.6), students might notice the connection to repeated addition through the +6 pattern or that all of the products are even or that the products are related to ×3 facts.

These tables can be extended to help students explore structure in computations with two-digit factors. To quickly multiply 6 × 13, 13 can be broken into 10 + 3, so 6 × 10 = 60 and 6 × 3 = 18, therefore 6 × 13 = 60 + 18, or 78. The table in Figure 8.7 shows multiplication by 6 with a two-digit factor and promotes discussions about patterns and the distributive property.

Figure 8.5 *Patterns and functions become clear when data is represented in a table.*

Number of flowers	1	2	3	4	5	6	7
Number of leaves	3	6	9	12	15	18	21

Figure 8.6 *Tables extend students' understanding of multiplication and division facts.*

Factor	1	2	3	4	5	6	7	8	9	10
×6 product	6	12	18	24	30	36	42	48	54	60

Figure 8.7 *By seeing the data in the table, students gain insights about multiplication with a two-digit factor.*

Factor	11 (10 + 1)	12 (10 + 2)	13 (10 + 3)	14 (10 + 4)	15 (10 + 5)	16 (10 + 6)	17 (10 + 7)	18 (10 + 8)	19 (10 + 9)	20 (10 + 10)
x6 product	66 (60 + 6)	72 (60 + 12)	78 (60 + 18)	84 (60 + 24)	90 (60 + 30)	96 (60 + 36)	102 (60 + 42)	108 (60 + 48)	114 (60 + 54)	120 (60 + 60)

Ratio tables are also perfect tools for exploring the structure of fractions. Look back at Figure 8.6 and think of the data as fractions equivalent to $\frac{1}{6}$. The organization of the table allows students to see and analyze a series of equivalent fractions. Students can quickly see that $\frac{2}{12}$ and $\frac{9}{54}$ are equivalent and that both can be simplified to $\frac{1}{6}$.

> Notice the use of models to gather data and the use of tables to organize the data so it is easier to analyze.

Give It a Try!

Using a fraction model, have students build a ratio table of fractions equivalent to $\frac{1}{2}$ and then discuss their observations of the data. Have them build a ratio table for other fractions like $\frac{1}{3}$, $\frac{1}{10}$, or $\frac{2}{3}$, using manipulatives, and always discuss their insights after looking at the data in their table. Can students build a ratio table for a different fraction (e.g., $\frac{1}{8}$, $\frac{1}{6}$, $\frac{3}{4}$) without using models? Can they apply the insights they gained from observing the previously made tables?

Connections
to other practice standards

Students model
mathematics as they
explore properties
(Standard 4).

Students look for
repetition to gain insight
into properties
(Standard 8).

Exploring Math Properties

A deep understanding of math properties (commutative, associative, distributive, identity) supports our students' computational skills. Whether working with math facts, multi-digit computations, or algebraic expressions, an understanding of these properties eases anxiety and simplifies math tasks.

EXPLORING THE COMMUTATIVE PROPERTY   Understanding the *commutative property* helps math facts make sense for our students. A number line can help our students visualize and prove that the order of the addends (or factors) does not affect the sum (or product). As students show that the sum of 9 + 6 is the same as the sum of 6 + 9 on a number line (see Figure 8.8), they are able to reach conclusions about the property.

Similarly, students can show equal jumps on a number line to prove this property with multiplication facts. Figure 8.9 shows 7 equal jumps of 4 and 4 equal jumps of 7. Both examples show that the product is 28.

Figure 8.8   *This student proves the commutative property using number lines.*

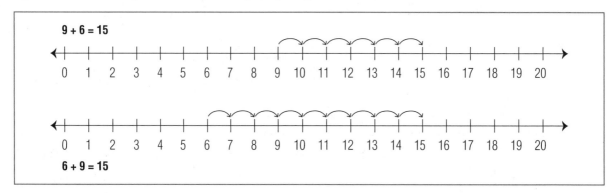

Figure 8.9   *Students use a double number line to prove the commutative property of multiplication.*

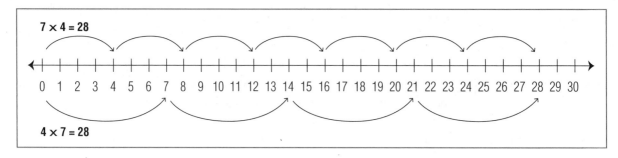

Digit cards and number line templates offer a great way to practice this concept. Students generate the numbers to add or multiply by selecting digit cards at random. Students write an equation for the numbers and then represent the equation on a number line. Students then write the commutative equation and represent it on another number line or on the bottom of their double number line.

EXPLORING THE DISTRIBUTIVE PROPERTY   The *distributive property* highlights the flexibility of numbers. When exploring multiplication facts like 7×8, students can break apart the 7 to 5 and 2 and compose new expressions of 5×8 and 2×8. Combining these known facts $(5 \times 8) + (2 \times 8) = 40 + 16 = 56$, they can find the solution to $7 \times 8 = 56$. Providing models can make this investigation visual as students use grid paper to make area models of 7×8 and area models of 5×8 and 2×8. The models can be placed together to prove that the products are equal (see Figure 8.10).

Figure 8.10   *This student uses models to explore and prove the distributive property.*

ADDITIONAL IDEAS FOR DEVELOPING THE PRACTICE

Do your students see the predictability of math? Do they recognize patterns and functions? Can they apply properties to solve problems and make sense of math ideas? Expand on what you are already doing with some of the suggestions below.

Our students are better able to . . .	Because as teachers we . . .
Look closely to discern a pattern or structure.	Consistently ask students, "What do you notice?" Explore patterns in different ways using hundred charts, addition and multiplication charts, ratio tables, place-value models, etc. Sort and classify shapes based on defining attributes (e.g., 3 sides, 3 vertices, similar angle measurements).

(continues)

Our students are better able to . . .	Because as teachers we . . .
Understand math properties and apply them to computations.	Provide investigations in which students explore math properties.
	Facilitate discussions about math properties.
	Provide models for the exploration of properties.
	Ask students to construct arguments to prove math properties.
	Use understanding of properties to help students perform computations with multi-digit numbers, fractions, decimals, etc.
See the flexibility of numbers.	Continually model the composing and decomposing of numbers and shapes.
	Ask students to model the breaking apart and putting together of numbers, including whole numbers, fractions, and decimals, etc.

ASSESSMENT TIP

Check students' understanding of patterns by asking them to complete and describe number patterns. Their descriptions will help you determine their level of understanding. The student in Figure 8.11 notices a pattern in the denominators of the fractions (doubling) and is able to successfully continue the pattern, but she does not notice how the fractional value changes. While we are happy that this student identified that the denominators were doubling, we also want her to recognize the pattern in the fractional value. This student's writing helps us identify the need for continued classroom discussions about the pattern related to the value of each fraction in the sequence.

Figure 8.11 *This student recognizes the pattern in the denominators (doubling), but does not mention a pattern related to the value of each fraction. The fractions are decreasing by half as the pattern continues.*

Look at the pattern below.

$\frac{1}{2}, \frac{1}{4}, \frac{1}{8}, \frac{1}{16}, \underline{\frac{1}{32}}, \underline{\frac{1}{64}}, \underline{\frac{1}{128}}$

Write the missing fractions. Tell how you knew which fractions to write.

because the denominators go from 2, 4, 8, 16
So the denominator is multiplyed by 2

Try some of the following patterns to see if your students can accurately identify and describe patterns:

Write the next 3 numbers in the pattern, then describe the pattern.

2, 4, 6, 8, _____, _____, _____

4, 8, 12, 16, _____, _____, _____

2, 5, 9, 14, _____, _____, _____

4, 8, 16, 32, _____, _____, _____

$\frac{1}{2}, \frac{1}{4}, \frac{1}{8}, \frac{1}{16},$ _____, _____, _____

.5, .65, .8, .95, _____, _____, _____

$\frac{1}{3}, 1, 1\frac{2}{3}, 2\frac{1}{3},$ _____, _____, _____

SUMMING IT UP

Math has structure. When our students understand the properties of math, see the patterns in math, and understand the flexibility of numbers, they are able to see math as predictable. Through these understandings about the structure of mathematics, math makes sense.

Exploring Standard 8: *Look for and Express Regularity in Repeated Reasoning*

WHY FOCUS ON REPETITION?

Mathematicians are observers. We notice repetition and try to make sense of it. We observe what happens repeatedly and then figure out rules or shortcuts so we can get to answers more quickly. When determining a 15 percent tip, we simply find 10 percent of the total bill and then add half more rather than doing the lengthier computation. It is a shortcut that always works. When we are looking for the area of the bedroom floor to buy carpeting, we simply measure the length and width and multiply them to find the area—no need to measure the whole floor, the formula will give us that information much more quickly. We find ways to minimize our efforts in mathematics through shortcuts that are the result of our observations and our ability to notice and make sense of repetition.

UNDERSTANDING THE STANDARD

In Standard 7, we explored the structure of mathematics. Patterns and properties make math predictable. When a discipline has structure, repetition occurs. And once our students recognize and analyze what they are seeing repeatedly, they discover shortcuts—like algorithms or formulas—to make the tasks easier. Kindergarten students notice repetition in the counting sequence, always following a 1 to 9 sequence. Once they recognize this, they are able to continue their counting with "twenty-one, twenty-two, twenty-three" and "thirty-one, thirty-two, thirty-three. . . ." Second-grade students use their repeated observations about breaking apart numbers to create a shortcut when adding 45 + 8, saying, "45 + 5 = 50 and I just added 3 more to make 53." Sixth-grade students notice that a rectangle can be split into two right triangles. If the area of a rectangle can be found by multiplying base × height, wouldn't the area of a right triangle be found with $\frac{1}{2}bh$? Our students gain insights and are able to understand and discover generalizations through their experiences with observations of repeated events.

Mathematically proficient students:

▶ notice repetition.

▶ discover shortcuts and generalizations.

EXPLORING REPETITION

Recognizing repetition, and then figuring out why it is happening, is an important reasoning skill. Mrs. Short's kindergarten students began exploring +1 with number lines. Mrs. Short rolled a number cube to generate a number, and partners added 1 to the number by showing it on their number line. Mrs. Short then recorded the number sentence on the board. Students repeated the process until the following was on the board:

K.OA.1

> *2 + 1 = 3*
>
> *5 + 1 = 6*
>
> *3 + 1 = 4*
>
> *6 + 1 = 7*
>
> *4 + 1 = 5*

Mrs. Short asked her students to look at the number sentences and to think about adding 1 on their number lines. They talked with their partners about what they noticed. Students were able to draw the conclusion that the answer was "the next number." Mrs. Short asked her students to use their idea to predict what would happen if they added 1 to 7. She then had them check their predictions using their number lines. She posed several more numbers, asking students to predict +1 and to check their predictions on their number lines. Her students were excited to be able to predict the answers using their new insight that +1 would be the next number in the counting sequence.

Mrs. Johnson posed the following problem to her third-grade students:

> *At the ice-cream shop, Sara could choose chocolate, vanilla, or strawberry ice cream. She could have hot fudge, cara- mel, or marshmallow topping. She ordered one scoop of ice cream and one topping. What are all of the ice cream/top- ping possibilities she could have ordered?*

Students were asked to work with partners to solve the problem. Mrs. Johnson noticed a number of pairs struggling to identify a strategy for solving the problem. She called a class time-out, asking students to turn their papers over for a minute so they could talk about strategies. "Does this problem remind you of any others we have done?" she asked. Students talked with partners and then shared some similar problems.

Kelly: It's like the one with the drinks and sandwiches.

Teacher: How is it like that one?

Kelly: There were lots of different ways you could do it.

Maddie: It's like the hot dog one, too—when we had different things to put on the hot dog and hamburger.

Teacher: What did we do to make those easier?

Ben: We wrote it down.

Rosie: We did one at a time. Like we did all the ketchup, then all the mustard.

Emma: We made a list.

Teacher: If this is a similar problem, could we use those ideas for this problem? Would it help us? Think about that as you get back to work.

Mrs. Johnson helped her students identify familiar problems, problems they had experienced that had similar qualities. The familiar problems helped them identify a possible plan for the new problem. In Chapter 1 we discussed the importance of students knowing a variety of strategies to solve problems. Identifying familiar prob- lems, by noticing the repetitive elements in similar problems, is a critical way that our students decide which strategy makes sense for a given problem.

5.NBT.7   Mr. Newell's fifth graders were multiplying decimals. He had them first estimate the answer and use their estimate to figure out where to place the decimal point. When multiplying 41.2×4.7, Tim said, "It is about 40×5, so the answer is about

200." When he multiplied and got 19,364, he decided to place the decimal point at 193.64 because it would be close to 200. After doing a series of similar decimal estimation and computation tasks, Tim noticed something interesting: "There were 2 numbers in decimal places before we multiplied and 2 numbers in decimal places in the answer! It keeps doing that." Mr. Newell asked, "Does that make sense? I wonder if that will always happen?" Mike thought it would because the "numbers to the left are the whole numbers we used to estimate." Mr. Newell asked his students to keep an eye out to see if that kept happening. Mr. Newell was encouraging the students to observe repetition and try to make sense of it.

Mr. O'Connell's seventh-grade students were exploring multiplication with integers. He provided students with integer number lines and asked them to work with partners to create and solve a repeated addition equation for:

7.NS.2

3×-5

Students talked with partners and shared $-5 + -5 + -5 = -15$, justifying their solutions on the number line. After they did several more as a class, discussing and justifying their findings, Mr. O'Connell had them work with partners to model and solve expressions as he observed them at work. Students recorded:

Expression	Repeated Addition Equation	Multiplication Equation
4×-3	$-3 + -3 + -3 + -3 = -12$	$4 \times -3 = -12$
2×-4	$-4 + -4 = -8$	$2 \times -4 = -8$
3×-6	$-6 + -6 + -6 = -18$	$3 \times -6 = -18$
5×-2	$-2 + -2 + -2 + -2 + -2 = -10$	$5 \times -2 = -10$

After asking them to defend their solutions, Mr. O'Connell asked them to observe their data.

▸ What did they notice about the signs of the sums and products?

▸ Did what they saw make sense?

▸ Would the product of a positive and a negative integer always be negative?

▸ Could they explain it?

After modeling with number lines, his students were able to see why the sums and products would be negative, and they were able to verbalize a rule. Jeremy explained,

"If one of the factors is negative it has to be a negative product because it is like you are adding a lot of negative numbers. It will always be negative." Heather agreed, "It keeps getting more negative if you add more negative numbers. We kept going left on the number line." The students discovered, and brought meaning to, the rule.

INVESTIGATIONS TO FIND SHORTCUTS

Throughout our school experiences, we were told to memorize many math rules without understanding why they worked. We were told that these were "tricks" to make math easier, but there are no "tricks" in math. It is understanding math that makes it easier. When our students discover rules or generalizations, they are making sense of mathematics. It builds a stronger foundation than simply accepting and memorizing someone else's rule. Setting up opportunities for our students to discover rules or generalizations allows them to exercise their reasoning skills as they are making sense of math concepts. And they are more likely to remember the rules and generalizations that they have discovered on their own!

1.OA.6

Mrs. King could simply have told her first-grade students that when you add 10 to any single-digit number, you just put a 1 in front of the number. Instead, she allowed her students to figure it out. She began an exploration by giving each student a piece of square paper and having them draw a circle on it to represent a cookie (O'Connell and SanGiovanni 2011). She had students spin a 1–9 spinner to find out how many chocolate chips would be in their cookies and asked them to write the number above their cookies and also draw that number of chocolate chips on their cookies.

"Would you like even more chocolate chips in your cookie?" she asked. Then she told her students that they could each add 10 more chocolate chips to their cookies, but they would need to figure out how many total chocolate chips were now in their cookies. She asked them to write a number sentence to show what happened when they added 10 more chips. Students drew the chips, added them, and created their number sentences. Once students had completed their investigation, she asked them to share their solutions with her as she recorded the solutions on the board (see Figure 9.1).

Mrs. King asked her students to look at their solutions. What did they notice? Did they see any patterns? Did they notice anything interesting about the solutions? Her students noticed the vertical patterns of adding 1 more and noticed that all of the number sentences contained a +10. She asked them to be sure they also looked across each number sentence. Brendan said, "The answer has a 1 in front of the number. It's the same number, just with a 1!" Mrs. King asked them to think about that 1.

Figure 9.1 *The teacher recorded the students' findings as they added 10 more chocolate chips to their cookies.*

$$1 + 10 = 11$$
$$2 + 10 = 12$$
$$3 + 10 = 13$$
$$4 + 10 = 14$$
$$5 + 10 = 15$$
$$6 + 10 = 16$$
$$7 + 10 = 17$$
$$8 + 10 = 18$$
$$9 + 10 = 19$$

"What does the 1 represent?" she asked. "It's in the tens place," Allison said. "It's a 10 and a 4 when it's 14," Bailey said. Mrs. King's students were making sense of the rule many of us were merely told: "When you add 10 to a single-digit number, just put a 1 in front of the number."

Mrs. Michaels could have told her third graders that you create equivalent fractions by multiplying the numerator and denominator by the same number, but instead she chose to set up an exploration. Students were placed in teams of four, and each team was given a recording sheet that was placed in the center of the team, along with another sheet that became their fraction model. One student folded the fraction paper in half, then took a yellow crayon and colored $\frac{1}{2}$ of the paper. One teammate wrote $\frac{1}{2}$ on the recording sheet to show the part of the paper that was yellow, then the person holding the fraction model passed it to the person on his right. That person folded it back in half and then in half again and opened it. Teams were asked to decide what fraction of the model was now yellow. Some students said $\frac{2}{4}$ and Mrs. Michaels had them justify their answers. Others said $\frac{1}{2}$. Mrs. Michaels questioned, "Is $\frac{1}{2}$ of the paper still yellow? Is $\frac{2}{4}$ the same as $\frac{1}{2}$?" She asked them to record $\frac{2}{4}$ on the recording sheet. "What sign should we place between them?" she asked. Students agreed on an equal sign and wrote $\frac{1}{2} = \frac{2}{4}$.

Mrs. Michaels then told the students to pass the fraction model to the person on their right and to do one more fold and open the paper. Students then discussed the fraction that was yellow and came up with $\frac{4}{8}$, $\frac{2}{4}$, and $\frac{1}{2}$. They recorded the new fraction and again used an equal sign. Their fraction models were passed to the right again,

3.NF.3

folded, and $\frac{8}{16}$, $\frac{4}{8}$, $\frac{2}{4}$, and $\frac{1}{2}$ were discussed. "Has the $\frac{1}{2}$ changed?" Mrs. Michaels asked. "Is it bigger? Smaller? Are these just different names we could call it?"

After generating a list of equivalent fractions, Mrs. Michaels asked her students to observe them. What did they notice? They talked about the numerators always being half of the denominators, which made sense since each fraction represented $\frac{1}{2}$. And they noticed that each new fraction was made by doubling the numerator and the denominator of the previous fraction ($\frac{1}{2} = \frac{2}{4}$ or $\frac{2}{4} = \frac{4}{8}$). Students created additional equivalent fractions by multiplying both the numerator and denominator by 2. Mrs. Michaels put $\frac{2}{2}$ on the board. "Is this what we are multiplying by?" she asked. As students explored $\frac{2}{2}$ and thought about multiplying by 1, they began to realize why all of the fractions still equaled $\frac{1}{2}$. They hadn't really changed the fraction by multiplying by 1.

The following day, Mrs. Michaels' plan was to have students fold the papers in thirds. What might they discover when they saw $\frac{1}{3} = \frac{3}{9} = \frac{9}{27}$? They were on their way to discovering more about equivalent fractions!

8.G.5 Mrs. Moran's eighth graders were exploring triangles. She supplied each pair with 6 triangles labeled 1–6. Students had previously worked on classifying triangles, based on sides or angles. For this lesson, Mrs. Moran asked them to work with their partners to use a protractor to measure the angles of each of their triangles, record each angle measurement, classify their triangle based on its angle measurements, and then find the sum of the angle measurements. Mrs. Moran moved through the room observing her students as they worked.

Figure 9.2 *This student investigates the angles of a triangle, finding that they form a straight line (180° angle).*

Following their investigation, students shared their measurements and classifications, as well as any observations based on their work. Students quickly recognized that the sum of the angles for all of their triangles was 180°. "I wonder if that is always true?" Mrs. Moran asked. Students began speculating and Mrs. Moran ended class with them wondering. Tomorrow, they would create their own triangles and cut each angle off to place them along a straight line (180°) as in Figure 9.2. Could they prove that it would always work?

HOW DO WE GET THERE?

CLASSROOM-TESTED TECHNIQUES

Organizing and Displaying Data to Discover Rules

In Chapter 8, we discussed tables as a way to organize data so it is easier to see patterns and functions, and ultimately, to discover insights. Whether we look horizontally or vertically at the table in Figure 9.3, we see the connections between the data and are able to make generalizations about those connections. With each new car, we add 4 more wheels (pattern + 4) or the number of wheels is 4 × the number of cars (function $4n$).

In Figure 9.4, a middle grades student explores the flying geese problem, creating a data table and graphing his data. He notices the linear function and determines that $2n + 1$ allows him to find the value for any step in the problem.

Connections
to other practice standards

Utilizing tables to identify and extend patterns or apply functions is a viable strategy for solving math problems (Standard 1).

The patterns or functions discovered from the table are critical data for building arguments (Standard 3).

Displaying data in an organized way is a model of the mathematics (Standard 4).

Figure 9.3 *Patterns and functions are evident as we look at the data in the table.*

Number of cars	1	2	3	4	5	6
Number of wheels	4	8	12	16	20	24

Figure 9.4 *This student visualizes his data in a table and on a graph and is able to explain the function he discovers (2n + 1).*

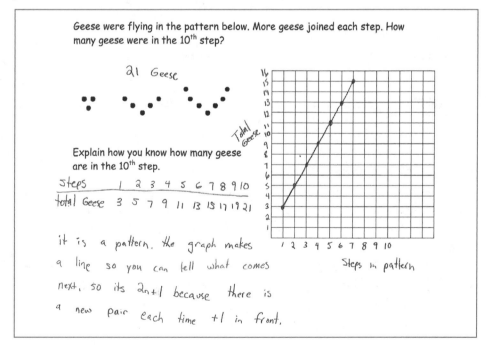

Pose problems in which students are challenged to extend patterns and look for a generalization, or algebraic relationship (function), to explain the pattern. For the example in Figure 9.3, we might ask, "How many wheels are needed for 20 cars?" Students who notice the $4n$ relationship can quickly solve the problem whether we are asking about 20, 200, or 2,000 cars.

1. Show 3 or 4 steps of a pattern.

2. Give students hands-on materials to explore and extend the pattern.

3. Have them tell you what comes next and why.

4. Have them record the data on a table.

5. For older students, have them graph the data and discuss what they observe.

Orchestrating Classroom Investigations to Discover Shortcuts

We've discussed the importance of students discovering math rules, generalizations, and shortcuts. Our goal is to set up investigations that allow them to have "ah-ha" moments. Some critical components of these investigations are

1. opportunities for all students to gather data with partners or teams.

2. creating compilations of class data.

3. observing compiled data and discussing insights.

Connections
to other practice standards

Students solve problems as they explore repetition in math (Standard 1).

Students use models (e.g., tables, lists, tree diagrams, etc.) to better understand repetition (Standard 4).

Students look for patterns and functions and generalize rules from their observations (Standard 7).

> **Give It a Try!**

Consider a class investigation like one of the following.

2.NBT.8

PLACE VALUE—ADDING 10 TO A THREE-DIGIT NUMBER Provide students with base-ten blocks and have them work with partners to create a model for a three-digit number (e.g., 347). Have them add 10 by adding 1 rod (ten) to their blocks and then counting the blocks to determine the new number (e.g., 357). Record both numbers on the board.

Do it again with a new three-digit number, having students create the number with blocks, add a rod (ten block), and determine the new number. After a number of examples are on the board (e.g., 347, 357, 632, 642, 974, 984, 275, 285 . . .), have partners observe the numbers to determine a rule for adding 10. (What happens to the number when we add 1 ten? Are we adding 1 to the tens digit? Does that make sense? Why or why not?) You can also try this activity with subtracting a ten or adding or subtracting a hundred.

FORMULA FOR DETERMINING THE NUMBER OF COMBINATIONS   Pose a problem similar to the following, but provide each team with different data (different numbers of sandwiches and drinks):

> *Jennifer wants to order a sandwich and a drink.*
>
> *There are 3 types of sandwiches (chicken, ham, tuna) and 2 types of drinks (milk and lemonade). How many different choices does she have?*

3.OA.1

Teams explore their problem and find their solution, then teams share their results. Record the data on the board.

Sandwiches	Drinks	Total combinations
3	4	12
2	4	8
5	2	10
3	3	9
2	3	6

Students observe the data to find a shortcut. (What do you notice? Can you find a shortcut? Why does your shortcut work? Does it make sense?)

FINDING PI   Have students work with partners to measure the circumference and diameter of a variety of circles and record the data. Have them find the ratio of the circumference to the diameter for each. Then have students make a scatter plot of the data with the horizontal axis representing diameters and the vertical axis representing circumferences. Have partners discuss their observations. Does the scatter plot produce a straight line? Is the slope close to 3.1?

7.G.4

ADDITIONAL IDEAS FOR DEVELOPING THE PRACTICE

Do your students notice repetition in numbers, measurement, probability, or geometry? Can they figure out why algorithms or formulas make sense? Are they developing an understanding of shortcuts and generalizations? Expand on what you are already doing with some of the suggestions below.

Our students are better able to . . .	Because as teachers we . . .
Notice repetition.	Ask students to observe for repetition. Frequently ask, "What do you notice?" "Do you see any patterns?" "Have we seen this before?" Pose problems that draw attention to repetition.
Select appropriate strategies for solving familiar problems.	Ask students to think about how new problems are like previously solved problems. Ask students to use familiar problems as a way to decide on an appropriate strategy.
Discover shortcuts or generalizations.	Set up investigations in which students gather data and observe for repetition in order to find shortcuts. Encourage discoveries. Ask students to explain shortcuts (formulas, algorithms). Compare shortcuts to other methods to see how they are alike and different.

ASSESSMENT TIP

Tasks that require students to gather data, organize that data, and look for patterns or functions would be appropriate assessments for this standard. Pose a problem to your students and ask them to solve and justify the problem. When analyzing their responses consider the following:

▸ Did they use an appropriate strategy to solve the problem?

▸ Did they gather and organize data as they solved the problem?

> ▸ Did they notice patterns or functions in the problem data?
> ▸ Were they able to justify their solution with data from the problem?

Primary

Erica was decorating gingerbread men with 2 raisins for eyes. How many raisins will she need to make 6 gingerbread men? Tell how you know.

Intermediate

Alice jumps rope faster than anyone in her class. She can jump 8 times in 4 seconds. How long will it take her to jump 40 times? Justify your answer.

Middle Grades

Mrs. Jones rented 8 square tables (only 1 person could fit at each side of the tables). She pushed the square tables together to form 1 long row of tables. How many guests could be seated with a row of 20 tables? Justify your answer.

Can you find a rule to tell you how many people could be seated for a row of n tables? Explain how you determined the rule.

SUMMING IT UP

Mathematicians are observant. They notice repetition and try to make sense of it. They organize data on tables, charts, and graphs so they can better analyze it. They look for insights and construct rules or generalizations to explain what they see. They use their insights to develop shortcuts like algorithms and formulas. Because of the structure of math, there is a lot of repetition. As our students notice repetition, and reason to understand why it is happening, they are making sense of math.

CHAPTER 10

Conclusion

Yes, another set of standards. These new standards have actually evolved over the past several decades, crafted from previous standards that value both the content and the process of mathematics. The CCSS content standards provide clear progressions of grade-level math content, and the Practice Standards provide the framework for putting that content into practice.

The eight CCSS Standards for Mathematical Practice intertwine with each of the CCSS content standards and impact all math teaching and learning, regardless of the skill or concept. It is through these eight Practices that students explore mathematics, build deeper understanding, develop reasoning, and learn to apply content knowledge to problem situations. They learn how to be mathematicians. And it is through these eight Mathematical Practices that we are guided to discover effective ways to teach mathematics in order to ensure that our students emerge from our classrooms with more than content knowledge, but with critical practices that will make them effective mathematicians.

The Standards for Mathematical Practice enlighten us to a new meaning of mathematical proficiency. We have readjusted our thinking to extend far beyond computational fluency to strive to support our students to become mathematical thinkers.

Appendix **A**
CCSS Standards for Mathematical Practice

1. Make sense of problems and persevere in solving them.

Mathematically proficient students start by explaining to themselves the meaning of a problem and looking for entry points to its solution. They analyze givens, constraints, relationships, and goals. They make conjectures about the form and meaning of the solution and plan a solution pathway rather than simply jumping into a solution attempt. They consider analogous problems, and try special cases and simpler forms of the original problem in order to gain insight into its solution. They monitor and evaluate their progress and change course if necessary. Older students might, depending on the context of the problem, transform algebraic expressions or change the viewing window on their graphing calculator to get the information they need. Mathematically proficient students can explain correspondences between equations, verbal descriptions, tables, and graphs or draw diagrams of important features and relationships, graph data, and search for regularity or trends. Younger students might rely on using concrete objects or pictures to help conceptualize and solve a problem. Mathematically proficient students check their answers to problems using a different method, and they continually ask themselves, "Does this make sense?" They can understand the approaches of others to solving complex problems and identify correspondences between different approaches.

2. Reason abstractly and quantitatively.

Mathematically proficient students make sense of quantities and their relationships in problem situations. They bring two complementary abilities to bear on problems involving quantitative relationships: the ability to *decontextualize*—to abstract a given situation and represent it symbolically and manipulate the representing symbols as if they have a life of their own, without necessarily attending to their referents—and the ability to *contextualize*, to pause as needed during the manipulation process in order to probe into the referents for the symbols involved. Quantitative reasoning entails habits of creating a coherent representation of the problem at hand; considering the units involved; attending to the meaning of quantities, not just how to compute them; and knowing and flexibly using different properties of operations and objects.

3. Construct viable arguments and critique the reasoning of others.

Mathematically proficient students understand and use stated assumptions, definitions, and previously established results in constructing arguments. They make conjectures and build a logical progression of statements to explore the truth of their conjectures. They are able to analyze situations by breaking them into cases, and can recognize and use counterexamples. They justify their conclusions, communicate them to others, and respond to the arguments of others. They reason inductively about data, making plausible arguments that take into account the context from which the data arose. Mathematically proficient students are also able to compare the effectiveness of two plausible arguments, distinguish correct logic or reasoning from that which is flawed, and—if there is a flaw in an argument—explain what it is. Elementary students can construct arguments using concrete referents such as objects, drawings, diagrams, and actions. Such arguments can make sense and be correct, even though they are not generalized or made formal until later grades. Later, students learn to determine domains to which an argument applies. Students at all grades can listen or read the arguments of others, decide whether they make sense, and ask useful questions to clarify or improve the arguments.

4. Model with mathematics.

Mathematically proficient students can apply the mathematics they know to solve problems arising in everyday life, society, and the workplace. In early grades, this might be as simple as writing an addition equation to describe a situation. In middle grades, a student might apply proportional reasoning to plan a school event or analyze a problem in the community. By high school, a student might use geometry to solve a design problem or use a function to describe how one quantity of interest depends on another. Mathematically proficient students who can apply what they know are comfortable making assumptions and approximations to simplify a complicated situation, realizing that these may need revision later. They are able to identify important quantities in a practical situation and map their relationships using such tools as diagrams, two-way tables, graphs, flowcharts, and formulas. They can analyze those relationships mathematically to draw conclusions. They routinely interpret their mathematical results in the context of the situation and reflect on whether the results make sense, possibly improving the model if it has not served its purpose.

5. Use appropriate tools strategically.

Mathematically proficient students consider the available tools when solving a mathematical problem. These tools might include pencil and paper, concrete models, a ruler, a protractor, a calculator, a spreadsheet, a computer algebra system, a statistical package, or dynamic geometry software. Proficient students are sufficiently familiar with tools appropriate for their grade or course to make sound decisions about when each of these tools might be helpful, recognizing both the insight to be gained and their limitations. For example, mathematically proficient high school students analyze graphs of functions and solutions generated using a graphing calculator. They detect possible errors by strategically using estimation and other mathematical knowledge. When making mathematical models, they know that technology can enable them to visualize the results of varying assumptions, explore consequences, and compare predictions with data. Mathematically proficient students at various grade levels are able to identify relevant external mathematical resources, such as digital content located on a website, and use them to pose or solve problems. They are able to use technological tools to explore and deepen their understanding of concepts.

6. Attend to precision.

Mathematically proficient students try to communicate precisely to others. They try to use clear definitions in discussion with others and in their own reasoning. They state the meaning of the symbols they choose, including using the equal sign consistently and appropriately. They are careful about specifying units of measure, and labeling axes to clarify the correspondence with quantities in a problem. They calculate accurately and efficiently, express numerical answers with a degree of precision appropriate for the problem context. In the elementary grades, students give carefully formulated explanations to each other. By the time they reach high school they have learned to examine claims and make explicit use of definitions.

7. Look for and make use of structure.

Mathematically proficient students look closely to discern a pattern or structure. Young students, for example, might notice that three and seven more is the same amount as seven and three more, or they may sort a collection of shapes according to how many sides the shapes have. Later, students will see 7×8 equals the well remembered $7 \times 5 + 7 \times 3$, in preparation for learning about the distributive property. In the expression $x^2 + 9x + 14$, older students can see the 14 as 2×7 and the 9 as $2 + 7$. They recognize the significance of an existing line in a geometric figure and can use the strategy of drawing an auxiliary line for solving problems. They also can step back for an overview and shift perspective. They can see complicated things, such as some algebraic expressions, as single objects or as being composed of several objects. For example, they can see $5 - 3(x - y)^2$ as 5 minus a positive number times a square and use that to realize that its value cannot be more than 5 for any real numbers x and y.

8. Look for and express regularity in repeated reasoning.

Mathematically proficient students notice if calculations are repeated, and look both for general methods and for shortcuts. Upper elementary students might notice when dividing 25 by 11 that they are repeating the same calculations over and over again, and conclude they have a repeating decimal. By paying attention to the calculation of slope as they repeatedly check whether points are on the line through $(1, 2)$ with slope 3, middle school students might abstract the equation $(y - 2)/(x - 1) = 3$. Noticing the regularity in the way terms cancel when expanding $(x - 1)(x + 1)$, $(x - 1)(x^2 + x + 1)$, and $(x - 1)(x^3 + x2 + x + 1)$ might lead them to the general formula for the sum of a geometric series. As they work to solve a problem, mathematically proficient students maintain oversight of the process, while attending to the details. They continually evaluate the reasonableness of their intermediate results.

Open-Ended Questions to Promote Problem Solving Teacher Bookmark

Open-Ended Questions to Promote Problem Solving

- Before
  - What is the question?
  - What data will help you find the solution?
  - How will you start to solve this problem?
  - Does this problem remind you of any others you have solved?
  - What did you do to solve that problem? Will it work here?

- During
  - Are you blocked? Should you try a new approach?
  - Does your answer make sense? Why or why not? If it doesn't make sense, what could you do?

- After
  - How did you solve the problem?
  - Why did you solve the problem that way?
  - What was easy/hard about solving this problem?
  - Where did you get stuck? How did you get unstuck?
  - Were you confused at any point? How did you simplify the task or clarify the problem?
  - Can you describe another way to solve the problem? Which way might be more efficient?
  - Is there another answer? Explain.

Appendix C

Broken Rulers

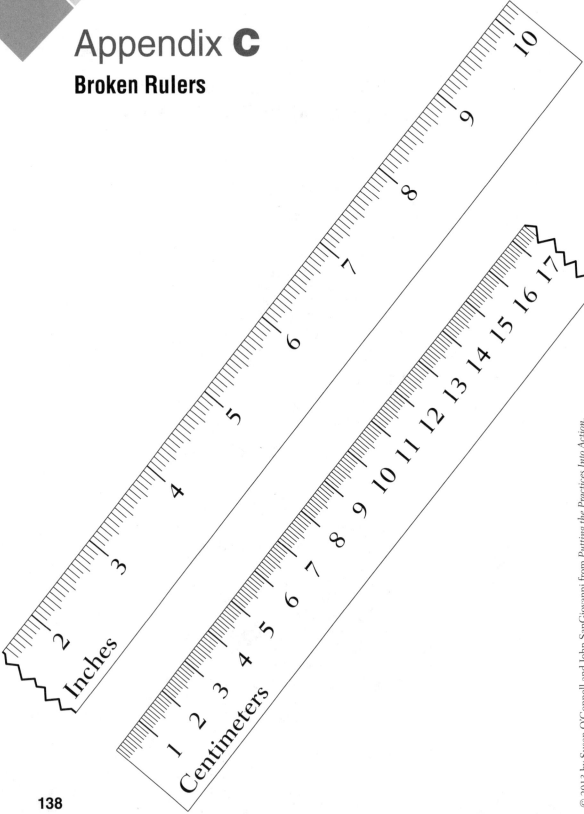

Appendix D
Sample Rich Tasks

R ich tasks, introduced in Chapter 2, require our students to think and act like mathematicians. They create a mathematics experience that integrates most, if not all, of the Standards for Mathematical Practice. These tasks may take more than one class period and offer many opportunities for extensions and variations. These tasks are about *doing* math.

Following are three rich tasks (primary, intermediate, and middle grades levels), including a series of before, during, and after questions to guide students' thinking throughout the task. Before the task, the teacher poses questions to set up the task. During the task, questions guide students' explorations. After exploring the task, questions facilitate the sharing of strategies and solutions, as well as provide optional extensions of the task. During these tasks, support your students with guiding questions, being cautious not to provide too much assistance, allowing students to think, explore, and learn.

Primary Task: *Helping Pets*

Following is a rich task in which students must determine solutions, of which there are many, with precisely 63 dogs and cats.

> *Three different veterinarians each help a total of 63 dogs and cats in a week, but each veterinarian helps a different number of dogs and cats. How many dogs and cats could each veterinarian have helped?*

Setting Up the Task

- ▸ What types of animals do people have as pets?
- ▸ What do we do when our pets get sick?
- ▸ What is a veterinarian?
- ▸ How many pets do you think a veterinarian can help in an hour or a day?
- ▸ What math is in this task? (Encourage students to come up with this, but the following questions may help if they get stuck.)
- ▸ How many dogs and cats do the three veterinarians help?
- ▸ Does each veterinarian help the same number of dogs or cats?

▶ What word do we use to describe the *total* number of dogs and cats?

▶ What is an *addend* in the problem? Will the addends be the same for each veterinarian?

Facilitating the Task

▶ How will you find the possible *addends* in this problem?

▶ What tools could you use to be sure you are accurate?

▶ How will you prove your solutions are correct?

▶ How will you explain your solutions to the class?

Extending the Task

▶ What are some of the solutions?

▶ Did we find all of the solutions? Are there more combinations of addends that have a sum of 63?

▶ How would our numbers change if each veterinarian also helped guinea pigs?

▶ How are the number of dogs and the number of cats related? What happens to the number of dogs when we decrease the number of cats?

Intermediate Task: *The Missing Puzzle Piece*

For this task, students should have had previous exposure to tangrams and know that there are 7 pieces of varied sizes and shapes in a set and that each set contains the same 7 pieces. The teacher arranges all 7 tangram pieces to form a design and traces its perimeter to create a puzzle. The teacher then gives each group of students a copy of the puzzle and a paper bag containing a set of tangrams, but with one piece randomly removed from each bag. The teacher tells the class that each group has one missing piece and challenges students to complete the puzzle to determine which piece is missing from their bag and then solve the following problem:

What fraction of your tangram puzzle is missing?

Setting Up the Task

▶ What types of puzzles have you worked with at school or at home?

▶ What are some strategies you have used to complete puzzles?

- ▸ What are tangrams? How many pieces are in a set?
- ▸ Are all of the pieces the same size and shape? What are the different shapes?
- ▸ What math is in this task? (Encourage students to come up with this, but the following questions may help if they get stuck.)
  - ▸ Will every piece represent the same fractional part? Why or why not?
  - ▸ What is one whole?
  - ▸ How do you think you can find the fractional piece that is missing?

Facilitating the Task

- ▸ What piece is your group missing? How do you know?
- ▸ How can you find the fractional amount of that piece?

Extending the Task

- ▸ What was your strategy for finding the missing piece? Did every group find the same piece missing?
- ▸ What piece was your group missing? What fractional part of the tangram set did that piece represent? How did you determine the fraction? (Have groups share their findings.)
- ▸ What if I placed two sets of tangrams in your bag and the same piece was missing from each set. Would the fraction change if that piece was missing from 2 sets of tangrams? How would it change?
- ▸ What if a third set of tangrams was added to your bag? How would the value of the missing piece change if it was the only piece missing in 3 sets of tangrams?
- ▸ Would the value change if there were a total of 4 sets of tangrams? Is there a pattern in the value of the missing piece and the number of sets used in the puzzle?

Connections
to other practice standards

The Missing Puzzle Piece is a problem-solving task (Standard 1).

This task requires students to justify their solutions and strategies (Standard 3).

Students use tangrams to model fractions (Standard 4) and also use them as tools as students find benchmarks and compare one tan to another to determine a fraction of the whole (Standard 5).

Precision is expected as students determine the fraction of the set that is missing (Standard 6).

The extension challenges students to look for patterns as they explore the changes if a piece were missing from 1, 2, 3, or 4 sets of tangrams (Standard 7).

—— **Middle Grades Task:** *Usable Classroom Floor Space* ——

Following is a rich task in which students must determine floor space in various classrooms and make judgments based on their findings:

> **Which mathematics classroom in our school has the greatest amount of usable floor space?**

Setting Up the Task

▸ What is floor space?

▸ How is floor space different from the total area of a classroom?

▸ Why is floor space important in any room, especially a classroom?

▸ What math is in this task? (Encourage students to come up with this, but the following questions may help if they get stuck.)

▸ What is the area of our classroom?

▸ What is the area of the floor space in our classroom?

▸ What is the area of other classrooms?

▸ What is the area of the floor space in those classrooms?

▸ Is it fair to say a larger classroom has a larger amount of floor space? Should we consider the overall size of the classroom in relation to its overall floor space (percentage of floor space)?

Facilitating the Task

▸ How will we find the area of our classroom?

▸ What tools will help us find the area of our classroom?

▸ What tools will help us find the area of the closets, tables, furniture, etc.?

▸ Will we need to find the area of every desk? How will we find the area of all the desks?

▸ Do we need exact measurements of each desk or table? What would "good" measurements be?

Extending the Task

▸ Which classroom had the greatest amount of floor space? Justify your answers.

▸ How could our classroom be rearranged to maximize the floor space?

▸ What room in your house has the most usable floor space?

References

National Council of Teachers of Mathematics. 1989. *Curriculum and Evaluation Standards for School Mathematics.* Reston, VA: National Council of Teachers of Mathematics.

————. 2000. *Principles and Standards for School Mathematics: An Overview.* Reston, VA: National Council of Teachers of Mathematics.

————. 2006. *Curriculum Focal Points for Prekindergarten through Grade 8 Mathematics: A Quest for Coherence.* Reston, VA: National Council of Teachers of Mathematics.

————. 2010. *Making It Happen: A Guide to Interpreting and Implementing Common Core State Standards for Mathematics.* Reston, VA: National Council of Teachers of Mathematics.

National Governors Association Center for Best Practices and Council of Chief State School Officers. 2010. *Common Core State Standards for Mathematics.* www.corestandards.org/assets/CCSSI_Math%20Standards.pdf (accessed on July 28, 2010).

National Research Council. 2001. *Adding It Up: Helping Children Learn Mathematics.* Washington, DC: National Academy Press.

O'Connell, Susan R. 2007a. *Introduction to Communication, Grades 3–5* (The Math Process Standards Series). Portsmouth, NH: Heinemann.

————. 2007b. *Introduction to Problem Solving, Second Edition, Grades 3–5* (The Math Process Standards Series). Portsmouth, NH: Heinemann.

O'Connell, S., and J. Sangiovanni. 2011. *Mastering the Basic Math Facts in Addition and Subtraction: Strategies, Activities, and Interventions to Move Students Beyond Memorization.* Portmouth, NH: Heinemann.

Polya, George. 2004. *How to Solve It: A New Aspect of Mathematical Method.* Princeton, NJ: Princeton University Press.

Teacher Resources

WEBSITES

CORE STANDARDS

www.corestandards.org/

The official website of the Common Core State Standards includes the standards, news, resources, and frequently asked questions.

ILLUSTRATIVE MATHEMATICS

http://illustrativemathematics.org/

Illustrative Mathematics provides guidance to states, assessment consortia, testing companies, and curriculum developers by illustrating the range and types of mathematical work that students experience in a faithful implementation of the Common Core State Standards, and by publishing other tools that support implementation of the standards.

ILLUMINATIONS WEBSITE

www.nctm.illuminations.org

The National Council of Teachers of Mathematics' *Illuminations* website contains many problem-based lessons that can be quickly accessed and easily downloaded. Lessons often include applets and are filled with teacher support, including a listing of key questions to build students' understanding. The activities and lessons on the site provide examples of the integration of process and content.

TEACHER RESOURCE BOOKS

For additional insights, meaningful tasks, and further elaboration on the teaching of math practices, consider the following resources.

THE MATH PROCESS STANDARDS SERIES (HEINEMANN, 2007–2008)

This series provides PreK–8 teachers with an in-depth understanding of the National Council of Teachers of Mathematics' Process Standards. Each book focuses on one of the critical processes of problem solving, reasoning, communication, representation, and connections that are foundational to the CCSS Standards for Mathematical Practice. Each book offers teaching ideas and a CD filled with classroom tasks for teachers wanting more ideas for developing these practices.

Introduction to Problem Solving

These books highlight practical techniques for helping students make sense of math problems, including teaching tips for developing a variety of problem-solving strategies, as well as problem tasks designed to help students develop the mathematical thinking necessary to solve a wide range of math problems.

O'Connell, S. 2007. *Introduction to Problem Solving, Grades PreK–2.* Portsmouth, NH: Heinemann.

O'Connell, S. 2007. *Introduction to Problem Solving, Second Edition, Grades 3–5.* Portsmouth, NH: Heinemann.

Schackow, J., and S. O'Connell. 2008. *Introduction to Problem Solving, Grades 6–8.* Portsmouth, NH: Heinemann.

Introduction to Representation

These books share ways to help students use graphs, manipulatives, diagrams, and other models to explore math concepts and make sense of math ideas.

Witeck, K., and B. Ennis. 2007. *Introduction to Representation, Grades PreK–2.* Portsmouth, NH: Heinemann.

Ennis, B., and K. Witeck. 2007. *Introduction to Representation, Grades 3–5.* Portsmouth, NH: Heinemann.

Ennis, B., and K. Witeck. 2008. *Introduction to Representation, Grades 6–8.* Portsmouth, NH: Heinemann.

Introduction to Communication

These books explore the power of talking and writing in the math classroom, with ideas for vocabulary development, teacher questioning, and constructing math arguments, along with practical strategies to help students put their ideas into words, clarify them, elaborate on them, and ultimately produce clear and organized math writing.

O'Connell, S., and K. O'Connor. 2007. *Introduction to Communication, Grades PreK–2*. Portsmouth, NH: Heinemann.

O'Connell, S. 2007. *Introduction to Communication, Grades 3–5*. Portsmouth, NH: Heinemann.

O'Connell, S., and S. Croskey. 2008. *Introduction to Communication, Grades 6–8*. Portsmouth, NH: Heinemann.

Introduction to Reasoning and Proof

These books present ways to help students explore their reasoning and support their mathematical thinking, including strategies for encouraging students to describe their reasoning about math activities.

Schultz-Ferrell, K., B. Hammond, and J. Robles. 2007. *Introduction to Reasoning and Proof, Grades PreK–2*. Portsmouth, NH: Heinemann.

Schultz-Ferrell, K., B. Hammond, and J. Robles. 2007. *Introduction to Reasoning and Proof, Grades 3–5*. Portsmouth, NH: Heinemann.

Thompson, D., and K. Schultz-Ferrell. 2008. *Introduction to Reasoning and Proof, Grades 6–8*. Portsmouth, NH: Heinemann.

Introduction to Connections

These books highlight the importance of encouraging children to develop understanding and insight by making connections between and among math concepts.

Bamberger, H., and C. Oberdorf. 2007. *Introduction to Connections, Grades PreK–2*. Portsmouth, NH: Heinemann.

Bamberger, H., and C. Oberdorf. 2007. *Introduction to Connections, Grades 3–5*. Portsmouth, NH: Heinemann.

Langrall, C., S. Meier, E. Mooney, with H. Bamberger. 2008. *Introduction to Connections, Grades 6–8*. Portsmouth, NH: Heinemann.

ADDITIONAL TEACHER RESOURCE BOOKS THAT
SUPPORT MATH PRACTICES

Chapin, S., C. O'Connor, and N. Anderson. 2003. *Classroom Discussions: Using Math Talk to Help Students Learn.* Sausalito, CA: Math Solutions.

Leinwand, S. 2009. *Accessible Mathematics.* Portsmouth, NH: Heinemann.

National Council of Teachers of Mathematics. 2010. *Making It Happen: A Guide to Interpreting and Implementing Common Core State Standards for Mathematics.* Reston, VA: National Council of Teachers of Mathematics.

National Council of Teachers of Mathematics. 2004. *Navigating Through Problem Solving and Reasoning.* Reston, VA: National Council of Teachers of Mathematics.

O'Connell, S., and J. SanGiovanni. 2011. *Mastering the Basic Math Facts in Addition and Subtraction: Strategies, Activities, and Interventions to Move Students Beyond Memorization.* Portsmouth, NH: Heinemann.

O'Connell, S., and J. SanGiovanni. 2011. *Mastering the Basic Math Facts in Multiplication and Division: Strategies, Activities, and Interventions to Move Students Beyond Memorization.* Portsmouth, NH: Heinemann.

Van de Walle, J., and L. Lovin. 2005. *Teaching Student-Centered Mathematics: Volume One, Grades K–3.* New York: Pearson.

Van de Walle, J., and L. Lovin. 2005. Volume Two, *Teaching Student-Centered Mathematics: Grades 3–5.* New York: Pearson.

Van de Walle, J., and L. Lovin. 2005. Volume Three, *Teaching Student-Centered Mathematics: Grades 5–8.* New York: Pearson.

Professional Learning Communities

Study Guide

GUIDING QUESTIONS

INTRODUCTION

1. What is the role of the Standards for Mathematical Practice in the CCSS?
2. How do these Practices relate to content standards?
3. Can these Practices be taught in isolation?
4. Why is it important for teachers to better understand these standards?
5. How will the understanding of these Practices impact math proficiency for your students?
6. How will the understanding of these Practices impact our math instruction?

CHAPTER 1: THE EVOLUTION OF STANDARDS-BASED TEACHING

1. What are the similarities and differences between the CCSS and the standards your school or district had been using?
2. In what ways had your school or district been emphasizing math processes (problem solving, communication, reasoning, representation, connections) rather than simply math content?
3. How will you become more familiar with the CCSS?

CHAPTER 2: EXPLORING STANDARD 1 MAKE SENSE OF PROBLEMS AND PERSEVERE IN SOLVING THEM

1. Why is problem solving now considered such a critical practice?
2. Why is it important for students to know many problem-solving strategies? How will you expand your students' repertoire of strategies?

3. How do you build positive attitudes about problem solving?

4. Consider the *Focus on the Question* activity:

   a. In what ways does the activity promote student engagement?

   b. In what ways does the activity promote discussion about math thinking?

   c. In what ways does the activity allow students to see others' thinking and gather new ideas?

   d. In what ways would the activity support struggling students as they develop their problem-solving skills?

5. Tape yourself during a problem-solving lesson. What types of questions do you ask?

CHAPTER 3: EXPLORING STANDARD 2 REASON ABSTRACTLY AND QUANTITATIVELY

1. Are your students able to build appropriate equations to solve math problems? In what ways do they struggle?

2. Do your students deeply understand math operations? How does this affect their ability to build equations?

3. In what ways would constructing word problems to match a given equation strengthen students' understanding of operations and equations?

CHAPTER 4: EXPLORING STANDARD 3 CONSTRUCT VIABLE ARGUMENTS AND CRITIQUE THE REASONING OF OTHERS

1. How does constructing arguments support deep understanding of math concepts?

2. How might you help students construct strong arguments?

3. Consider the *Eliminate It* activity:

   a. What vocabulary terms or concepts would you want to use in your classroom?

   b. What numbers or expressions would prompt rich discussion in your classroom?

4. What are the benefits of students listening to and critiquing each other's arguments?

5. How might you help students effectively critique math arguments?

CHAPTER 5: EXPLORING STANDARD 4 MODEL WITH MATHEMATICS

1. What manipulatives are accessible to your students?

2. Do your students have access to electronic manipulatives? How might these enhance your teaching and/or your students' learning?

3. How might your students' modeling of math ideas be used as a formative assessment?

4. Consider the *Model It* activity:

    a. What are some concepts you are currently teaching that students should represent with models?

    b. What are different models you and your students can use for the topic you are currently teaching?

CHAPTER 6: EXPLORING STANDARD 5 USE APPROPRIATE TOOLS STRATEGICALLY

1. What math tools should your students be able to use effectively? Can they use those tools? If not, how will you help them build their skills?

2. In what ways can you help your students learn to select tools that are appropriate to specific tasks?

3. How might you help your students distinguish between the use of paper/pencil, mental math, and calculators when performing a computational task?

CHAPTER 7: EXPLORING STANDARD 6 ATTEND TO PRECISION

1. Are your students able to speak the language of math? In what ways do you help them understand the words of math?

2. What math vocabulary is critical to the current content you are teaching? How will you support your students in understanding these terms?

3. Why might word walls be a helpful addition to all math classrooms?

4. What terms will you include on your word wall? If you have students create word webs, what connections might they make?

5. Do your students understand the symbols of math? How might you assess their understanding?

6. Consider the *Estimate or Exact* activity:

   a. What computations have your students done recently that would have been good opportunities to estimate before finding the solution?

   b. What are some computations connected to the math concepts you are currently teaching? What types of estimation questions might you ask about those problems? (i.e., For 3.5 + 17.1, will our sum be greater than or less than 20?)

CHAPTER 8: EXPLORING STANDARD 7 LOOK FOR AND MAKE USE OF STRUCTURE

1. In what ways do patterns appear in your math lessons? Do your students routinely recognize patterns?

2. Do your students understand the properties of math? How will you support them to develop a deeper understanding?

3. In what ways do recognizing patterns and functions support students to be better able to solve math problems?

CHAPTER 9: EXPLORING STANDARD 8 LOOK FOR AND EXPRESS REGULARITY IN REPEATED REASONING

1. Do your students notice repetition in math? Give some examples.

2. In what ways can you help your students develop math rules or generalizations?

3. How does the recognition of familiar problems support students in choosing appropriate problem-solving strategies?

CHAPTER 10: CONCLUSION

1. What are the most significant contributions of the Standards for Mathematical Practice?

2. What might be the result if schools focus on content standards alone?

3. How will you ensure that Math Practices receive adequate attention in your classroom?